UNUSUAL PUBS
BY BOOT, BIKE AND BOAT

150 extraordinary licensed premises to visit around Britain

BOB BARTON

HALSGROVE

First published in Great Britain in 2017
Copyright © Bob Barton 2017

British Library Cataloguing-in-Publication Data
A CIP record for this title is available from the British Library

ISBN 978 0 85704 305 4

HALSGROVE
Halsgrove House,
Ryelands Business Park,
Bagley Road, Wellington, Somerset TA21 9PZ
Tel: 01823 653777   Fax: 01823 216796
email: sales@halsgrove.com

Part of the Halsgrove group of companies
Information on all Halsgrove titles is available at: www.halsgrove.com

Printed in India by Parksons Graphics

Opposite: *The Bounty, beside the Thames at Bourne End,
Buckinghamshire can only be reached by boot, bike or boat (see page 28).*

CONTENTS

The Fat Cat, Norwich is filled with old pub and brewery signs and has a superb range of ales and ciders (page 107).

ACKNOWLEDGEMENTS

TO TRAVEL AROUND this beautiful country researching pubs has hardly been the most arduous of tasks but this book would not have been possible without the help of a select band of individuals. I must thank my daughters, Caroline and Joanna, for being great company on various pub visits (including those on canal-boat holidays) and sometimes providing their own transport. Also James Young and John Weale for suggesting entries and accompanying me on numerous forays (our trips around Greater Manchester being particularly memorable); also with David Clarke into deepest Staffordshire. Thanks go to Graham Morrissey for driving a circuitous pub crawl through Wales. Other pleasant excursions have been in the company of Richard Tippett and Sue Adie, who I salute for her patient proof-reading of my sometimes erratic copy. Some pub suggestions have come from Jeremy Brinkworth and Andrew Daines.

Jacki Winstanley, Marketing Officer at Beamish, kindly facilitated my visit to the museum's superb Sun Inn. Thank you to the staff of Fuller's Parcel Yard at King's Cross, who allowed me to spend time taking many shots for the composite photograph of their pub's lofty atrium that appears alongside its entry in the Gazetteer; and staff and volunteers at the Black Country Living Museum, Dudley for creating and manning their early 1900s High Street so enthusiastically. I'd be happy to have the Bottle and Glass as my local.

I would like to say 'cheers' to the editors of the various regional magazines from the Campaign for Real Ale (CAMRA) – too many to list here – who have provided me with a steady flow of news and inspiration. Most of all, this book, which highlights a mere fraction of Britain's stock of wonderful hostelries, is a tribute to the regular pub-goers who keep them in business. Plus, of course, the licensees of the establishments featured, who work tirelessly providing hospitality.

Bob Barton, Hayes, Middlesex

PHOTOGRAPHIC CREDITS

INTRODUCTION

THERE ARE MANY pub guides that will tell you about beer selections, wine lists and menus but those concentrating on unusual, peculiar or odd establishments are rare. The plaudits received for my first book, *Unusual Railway Pubs, Refreshment Rooms and Ale Trains* (Halsgrove, 2013) inspired me to go in search of more locations, this time without the railway theme but with a wider range of peculiarities or eccentricities. These feature in the Gazetteer, which is a personal selection of 150 remarkable hostelries open for business (at press date).

So, what qualifies a place as unusual? It may be an unexpected location, out-of-the-ordinary decor, a notable feature or collection or surprising architecture. Sometimes a combination of these. A few are historical buildings – in one case on a consecrated site, i.e. a graveyard. Some were built to resemble castles, a medieval manor house or even a pack of playing cards but were always designed primarily for carousing.

In many years of pub visiting – and leisure travel generally – I have discovered the truth of the old saying 'the journey is the reward'. Getting to places of refreshment can be as much fun as sampling them. In that spirit, I have added the sub-title 'by boot, bike and boat' and, where appropriate, included basic information for walkers, cyclists and boat lovers. Hopefully, this will make the content more useful for followers of these pursuits and assist the planning and enjoyment of days out.

In the pages before the Gazetteer is a chapter putting Unusual Pubs in context. It looks at the beginnings of 'pubs with peculiarities', how people's concept of them has changed through the centuries and attempts to answer a question unlikely to appear on any syllabus: 'What is an Unusual Pub?'

In some ways, every pub in the country qualifies as Unusual. Thanks partly to variables such as customers, landlord, the staff, location and other vagaries – such as the prevailing weather, local events and traditions – no two are alike. Each is an experience that changes with every visit: one of the things that makes the British pub so special. Writing an elegy on the subject, titled *Time, gentlemen* (*The Economist,* December 16, 2010) the obituaries editor of the magazine summed it up eloquently:

'A pub can become a sort of encapsulation of place, containing some small turning's grainy photographs, its dog-eared posters for last year's fête, its snoozing cats, its prettiest girls behind the bar and its strangest characters in front of it... They hold ghosts, myths, the memory of kings; Green Men live on in them, White Horses carry Saxon echoes, Royal Oaks keep the drama of civil war and restoration.'

To that noble list I add: quirky architecture, wacky collections of memorabilia, unexpected locations and decidedly odd artefacts. Welcome to the wonderful world of Unusual Pubs...

Opposite: *The diminutive bar counter at the Circus Tavern, Manchester is under the stairs and George Best stood beside it. It's known as 'the smallest bar in Europe' (page 100).*

1. 'THERE'S NOTHING FOR YOU HERE!'

Musings on Unusual Pubs

I WOULD HAVE loved to have visited the Unusual Pub that featured the inept Henry (Michael Palin) and Albert (Terry Jones) as publicans, in the slapstick short film *Henry Cleans Up* (1974). In attempting to serve a customer a pint of beer, Henry manages to get his hand stuck in a glass washing machine, demolish a stack of beer bottles and pull down a shelf full of wine glasses in quick succession, shortly before his wife Doris spills a jug of water over him. Henry is mentored by Albert, the smarmy landlord of a nearby boozer, showing how things should be done – when he's not attending 'judo classes' with Henry's wife. People would pay to be entertained in a pub like that, especially with actors from *Monty Python's Flying Circus* behind the bar. (The film was an instructional one made for Guinness, showing their licensees, in an entertaining fashion, how to maintain beer lines and dispensers.)

A real, rather than a fictional, Unusual Pub I missed, because it closed before I started my travels, was the Escape, in Mabledon Place, off London's Euston Road. In the mid-1960s, this Whitbread house was decorated with barbed wire and mannequins in military uniforms, along with displays of artefacts connected with escapes from World War II prisoner-of-war camps. There were forged documents, handmade concealment devices and other items that facilitated daring dashes from Stalag Luft III and the like. The full-size 'dummy POW', used during roll-call to give your escaping chum extra time to make a getaway before he was missed, was particularly ingenious. What made the hostelry extra special was that members of the Royal Air Forces' Escaping Society met there regularly, so you could enjoy a pint while being regaled with stories of secret plots, tunnels under the enemy's noses and thrilling getaways by the men who planned and executed them.

I started work as a fresh-faced teenager near London's Fleet Street in the early 1970s. My colleagues there introduced me to the twin pleasures of pub going and ale drinking. After growing up in a suburban beer desert in South Harrow – with non pub-going parents – it came as a revelation. I've been hooked on the bonhomie of licensed premises ever since. My baptism in pub-going was at the Old King Lud on Ludgate Circus, situated a couple of minutes from St Paul's Cathedral but replaced by a chain restaurant years ago. It was lunchtime and the place was busy with office workers, buzzing with conversation and laughter, and customers jostled for service at the bar. Cigarette smoke filled the air and brogues shuffled on bare floorboards. Not long afterwards, I was taken to my first Unusual Pub, the Black Friar, adjacent to Blackfriars Bridge. I was awe-struck by the extravagant marble and mahogany decoration and the fact that this ornate, Bacchanalian place seemed, at first glance, to be part of a monastery. Closer inspection revealed the devout friars depicted in the decorative features to be enjoying worldly pleasures of an epicurean nature. The Black Friar is an Edwardian architectural joke that has stood the test of time (the pub was built on the site of a Dominican friary) and is one of London's lesser known tourist attractions (see page 78).

When did pubs and inns start trading on their curiosities? The answer is probably as long ago as these places of refreshment have existed. The well-known Ye Olde Trip to Jerusalem in Nottingham attracts customers thanks to it being built partly into a cliff and its history, including being a supposed gathering or recruiting place for Crusaders heading to

Ye Olde Trip to Jerusalem, one of England's oldest pubs, has a warren of rooms carved out of Nottingham Castle's cliff.

at Defford (page 48) is a precious survivor and you are urged to go while there is still the chance. Similarly, bar counters are a comparatively recent invention not seen in licensed premises until the railway age. You can still be served with beer the old-fashioned way, often poured from a jug in a hostelry without a proper bar, at a small number of places such as the Dyffryn Arms, Pontfaen (page 112).

Conversely, some features considered unremarkable today would have been rare, if not unusual, in the distant past. A huge fire blazing in a large hearth – or a big bed well protected from draughts – would have been very special attractions in a medieval alehouse. Peter Clark, in *The English Alehouse a Social History* (Harlow, Longman, 1983) observes on page 66:

'In the winter time new arrivals went there at once to
warm themselves... A fire was a luxury for many poorer
people, badly dressed, sometimes without shoes and

The Fleece Inn at Bretforton, Worcestershire is known for its 'witches' circles', thought to protect the building from evil spirits entering down the chimneys (page 29).

fight in the Holy Land. Ye Olde Fighting Cocks in St Albans (page 117) has long drawn thirsty visitors from the nearby abbey thanks to its peculiar octagonal shape as much as its ale. Both lay claim to be the country's oldest pub. The Ostrich Inn, Colnbrook, which claims to be the third oldest inn (page 45), has long made an attraction out of an early landlord's penchant for murdering his customers, using an ingenious tipping bed. Probably ever since that rogue's trial and execution, in fact. Pilgrims from Chaucer's time, on the road to Canterbury, were recommended certain inns, no doubt, on the basis of their religious artefacts or extraordinary entertainment.

Some establishments were not at all unusual in the past but their rarity has made them so today. The simple rural ale or cider house – an ordinary domestic dwelling with no extra facilities for customers – was once ubiquitous. The Cider House

often lacking any heating at home. Frequently strangers wanting to stay the night would bunk down on the kitchen table or move into the landlord's room, sometimes joining him and his wife in bed.'

The ancient and historic George Inn at Norton St Philip (page 106) would have made it into a book of unusual pubs 600 years ago, thanks to its sheer size and involvement in the lively cloth fairs held in and around it. So would the pub in Kent created in the eighteenth century by eccentric landowner Lord Holland. Now called the Captain Digby, it looks like a castle and was built to entertain his guests (page 33). The Victorian Bristolian who turned part of his tavern into a representation of a tramcar (the King's Head, page 32) unwittingly created an early theme pub.

By late Victorian times, canny brewers and distillers were spending a fortune creating destination pubs with a 'wow' factor. This was the era of the Gin Palace, when no expense was spared on decoration that combined ornate tiling, engraved glass, mirrors and elaborate gas lighting, to take customers' breath away. In *Man Walks Into a Pub* (Pan Macmillan, 2010) author Pete Brown quotes a Victorian description of city gin palaces:

'At one place I saw a revolving light with many burners playing most beautifully over the door of the painted charnel house [this pejorative term is used to show the writer's disapproval]; at another, 50 or 60 jets in one lantern were throwing out their capricious and fitful but brilliant gleams as if from the branches of a shrub. And over the doors of a third house were no less than three enormous lamps with corresponding lights, illuminating the whole street to a considerable distance.'

Then there were the music halls, which started in the eighteenth century and soon became commonplace. Enterprising tavern and coffee house proprietors used the bait of cheap and cheerful entertainment to lure customers. Rooms devoted to musical clubs became quasi-theatres complete with stages, scenery and private boxes for certain members of the audience. They were often rowdy: tough venues in which to

perform. Items such as fruit, bottles and metal rivets would be hurled at acts that were disapproved of and, in some places, the orchestra had to be protected from missiles with a mesh stretched across their 'pit'. Wilton's in London, which evolved from a Victorian sailors' pub, is the 'world's oldest surviving grand music hall' and retains a delightful bar room (page 98).

In days past, a clever grouping of otherwise unlinked pubs could become a tourist attraction. An example is the Plumstead Common Idlers, a group of public houses near the eponymous common in Greenwich, south east London. An anonymous wit in the early 1900s (possibly earlier) observed that the Prince of Wales was 'the prince that never reigned,' while among other local taverns, the Star never shone, the Ship never sailed, the Old Mill was the mill that never turned (though the remains of a windmill stand beside it) and the Woodman never chopped. Finally, there's the pub named Who'd a Thought It (definition: an expression of surprise at a fact or statement). No doubt this early form of marketing consortium provided an excuse for many a pub crawl, accompanied by a picnic on the common, though there was nothing extraordinary about the public houses themselves. Apart from the first named and the Woodman, all are still hostelries.

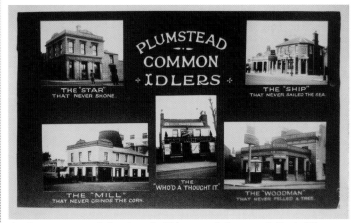

A vintage postcard showing the 'Plumstead Common Idlers'. They were four pubs that didn't live up to their names and another called the Who'd a Thought It?

Telephone box being used as a 'pop-up' pub by the villagers of Long Crendon, Buckinghamshire, in 2015.

Private 'pubs', created by enthusiasts in their homes or sheds, though undoubtedly quirky, are outside the realm of this book. So are establishments overseas, though deserving of a mention is the country inn run by British expat Ian Thurston. He had the surplus contents of the Sussex Arms, Tunbridge Wells shipped to his pub in Australia when it was refurbished in 2007 (*Metro*, 25 June, 2015). The website of the Fox and Hounds near Brisbane claims it is 'the only pub in Australia to have been transported from England.'

'Pop-up' pubs, where church halls, barns or redundant buildings are converted temporarily, often for charity or publicity, have become popular in recent years. Perhaps the most unusual are those set up in the restricted confines of a telephone box. Many of the Gilbert Scott designed 'K6' kiosks, dating from 1936, are now surplus to the requirements of BT and are being sold to local parish councils for as little as one pound. The Buckinghamshire village of Long Crendon is one example, opening a pub inside its box during 2015. Despite its small size, it stocked real ale, supplied by the local XT Brewing

Company and was fully 'engaged' with its customers. It wasn't the first telephonic pub.

Four years earlier, in July 2011, BBC Cambridgeshire reported that the villagers of Shepreth had turned their redundant 'phone box into a local, the Dog and Bone (Cockney rhyming slang for telephone). It was a one-night stunt to protest against the nearby Plough being turned from a public house into a private one. A triangular shaped bar counter was fitted inside the open door, with room for a barmaid inside who would draw beer from a cask beneath the counter. In the age of the micropub, perhaps there is scope for this idea to be developed on a permanent basis.

A few words about unusual inn signs. From the late Middle Ages the most common device to advertise a beerhouse was a pole with a bush hanging at the end, indicating that brewing had taken place. Unusual signs existed even then, according to Peter Clark in *The English Alehouse, a Social History,* such as a 'human hand made of wood and hanging at the end of a wand.' This type of sign was stipulated by Chester magistrates in 1573 when alcoholic drink was sold. Though I have been unable to find a disembodied hand advertising a pub in twenty-first century Britain, I have stumbled upon a full-size Post Office bicycle hung above The Postie in Royston (page 116); and a miniature steam locomotive emerging from the wall of the Railway Arms in Alton, Hampshire. A more conventional sign exhibiting a sense of humour is a caricature of actor Sid James from the *Carry On* films, at the Black Horse in Iver, Buckinghamshire. Pinewood Studios, where the comedy series was filmed, is nearby.

Not a sign as such, but an

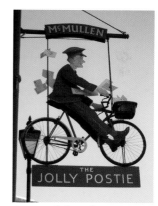

On your bike: The Jolly Postie's inn sign uses an ex-Royal Mail bicycle. Other postmen's cycles feature inside and around the garden of Royston's former post office.

Above: *The Railway Arms in Alton, Hampshire has a steam locomotive coming out of its front wall. There are level crossing-style gates in the rear garden.*

Left: *Losing face: One of the carved faces depicting the 'eight stages of drunkenness' on the fascia of the Last Orders, Blyth.*

has closed, possibly permanently but its Grade II listing should protect both building and sign. One that *is* open is the Magpie at Stonham Parva, Suffolk, which still has its 'gallows' sign across the road. According to members of CAMRA's Suffolk branch, within living memory there was also a live magpie billeted in a cage outside: a living pub sign. In York, the Olde Starre Inne in Stonegate needs its street-spanning sign as the hostelry is hidden in a medieval snickelway. It claims to be the

Huntsmen, along with a fox and hounds, cross above the road at the Fox and Hounds in the Hertfordshire village of Barley.

unusual exterior feature, is a series of eight carved comedic faces set into the fascia of the Last Orders (formerly The Railway) in Blyth, Northumberland. They depict a man as he descends from a sober state to a dishevelled, intoxicated one. The so-called 'eight stages of drunkenness' are not the sort of thing that modern pubs would care to advertise. In the early twentieth century, in former industrialized areas such as this – where workers would sink several pints daily to stay hydrated – it was seen as a way of promoting the establishment's quality ale.

Signs spanning the street were once quite common but are now unusual. A pub I was hoping to include in the Gazetteer was the Fox and Hounds in the Hertfordshire village of Barley. It has a sign, erected around 1955 but replacing a much earlier one, that emerges from the right-hand gable and straddles the road. Galloping across it are painted huntsmen and hounds, merrily chasing a fox towards the building. Sadly, the business

A vintage postcard depicting the 'gallows' sign at the Magpie in Stonham Parva, Suffolk. It is still a feature today, though there is no longer a caged magpie.

city's oldest licensed inn.

I have avoided including pubs that are 'record breaking', such as the largest, highest, tallest or have the most hand-pumps or toilet cubicles. Record holders are transitory and usually highly contentious. The Nutshell in Bury St. Edmunds (page 37) long held the record for being the smallest pub but this is now questionable due to the proliferation of micropubs. It deserves its place within these pages, however, because of its history of exhibiting unusual artefacts. The most bizarre was, and still is, a mummified cat, retrieved from a local building where it had been walled up. The tradition of pubs exhibiting collections of curiosities was started in the Victorian era, the Nutshell's being an attraction established by 1884. An advertisement of the period proclaimed

'Museum of Art and Curiosities.

The "Nutshell" Inn.

John H. Stebbing

While thanking his numerous friends and patrons for their support he has received during the eleven years he has been at the above residence, begs to intimate that he is continually adding to his large and varied

Collection of Antiquities, Which are well worth a visit.

Relics from the Late Wars and Ancient Relics from all Parts of the Globe.

The most unique and prettiest bar in the town.'

For those who seek out record breaking pubs, I suggest visiting J.D. Wetherspoon's Moon Under Water in Manchester's Deansgate and Ye Olde Cock Tavern in London's Fleet Street. Then let me know whether you agree that they have the largest floor area in the country and the narrowest street frontage in the capital respectively, as is often claimed. Unfortunately, the pub that claimed to have the longest name – situated at the end of a Victorian terrace in Stalybridge, Greater Manchester – closed in 2016. The Old Thirteenth Cheshire Astley Volunteer Rifleman Corps Inn is not a moniker that trips off the tongue easily, especially after a pint or two, so locals abbreviated it to the Rifleman. The band of soldiers to which it

Ye Olde Cock Tavern in Fleet Street is said to boast the narrowest street frontage in London.

refers was disbanded at the end of WWI but the place had a small cabinet of military artefacts to admire. A sad loss.

The anti-alcohol movement established in the nineteenth century created a new word – teetotal. It led to the opening of numerous coffee taverns and temperance bars where only non-alcoholic drinks were sold. Only one of the latter survives, a Victorian establishment called Fitzpatrick's in the Lancashire town of Rawtenstall. With its ceramic tap barrels and shelves

The Old Thirteenth Cheshire Astley Volunteer Rifleman Corps Inn, Stalybridge, had the longest pub name in the country. It closed in 2016.

lined with jars of medicinal herbs, it is little changed. I invite you to go along for a cup of sarsaparilla or dandelion and burdock and decide for yourself whether it qualifies as an Unusual Pub.

Though pubs are primarily places for harmless pleasure, like most of mankind's enjoyable pastimes, they have been used for nefarious activities too. Does the fact that the Blind Beggar in London's Whitechapel has a plaque denoting that gangster Ronnie Kray shot George Cornell of the Richardson gang there classify it as unusual? Similarly, does the reputation that the Star Tavern in London's Belgravia was used for meetings of some of the Great Train Robbery gang (£2.6 million stolen from a Glasgow to London mail train in 1963) make it extraordinary? More recently, there is the Castle in Islington, where criminals who executed the £14 million Hatton Garden deposit box heist of 2015 met. 'Britain's biggest ever burglary was planned in a pub with help from a book called *Forensics for Dummies*, a court was told' – ran the story in *Metro* on 24 November that year.

Another pub was infamous for its link to a crime of passion. The frontage of the Magdala, near London's Hampstead Heath, reputedly bears bullet holes from the 1955 shooting, by Ruth Ellis, of her lover David Blakely. The wood-panelled interior included an informative exhibit about the crime. Ellis was the last woman to be executed in Britain and public outrage fuelled by her hanging was instrumental in the abolition of the death penalty. The Magdala closed (for a second time) in early 2016 and its future is uncertain.

Pubs do not necessarily need to look strange or be full of peculiar objects to be classified as unusual. Other than the fact it faces a canal rather than a road, the Rising Sun in Berkhamsted (page 22) *looks* like a perfectly ordinary pub. The Riser's unusualness tends to sneak up on you. Alongside its range of real ales and ciders, it sells snuff and exotic liqueurs. It has biscuits on the bar for dogs – and often hands out free snacks to humans too. But woe betide those who don't bring their own cheese to its cheese club. Events include boules games, open-air theatre, community choir singing – and work parties to paint the adjacent canal lock. Once a month there's a

Pub with no beer: Fitzpatrick's in Rawtenstall is Britain's last temperance bar.

The Ship and Shovell is a pub on both sides of the same street— namely Craven Passage, near London's Charing Cross. The two buildings share a common cellar.

pop-up gastronomic experience, 'Fanny's Restaurant'. It is what people call a 'proper pub' – but with added eccentricity. A poster outside shows the Local Shop from BBC television's black comedy *League of Gentlemen*, its caption advising 'There's nothing for you here.'

One of the factors that motivated me to write this book was that it will, hopefully, inspire more pub visits. They have been closing at a frightening rate – the Institute of Economic Affairs says the UK has lost 21,000 pubs since 1980, with half of these closures taking place since 2006 (*Closing Time – Who's Killing the British Pub?*, Christopher Snowdon, December 2014). CAMRA claims 29 a week are being lost nationally (*London Drinker*, December-January 2015-16). At that pace, the last pub in Britain will ring last orders in 2049, says the article. Though that apocalyptic scenario is unlikely – and CAMRA reported

the net number of pubs closing per week had fallen to 21 in summer 2016 – the warnings should not be ignored. In this age of cut-price supermarket alcohol, competing leisure-time entertainment and ever more diverting digital gadgets, we need to realise that once traditional pubs are lost they can never be replaced.

Any old iron: At the Crate Brewery in Hackney, the bar counter is made from railway sleepers, while lampshades have been created from bedsprings and old chains. Pallets and warehouse trolleys have become seats and tables (page 81).

LOCATIONS WITH FEATURED PUBS

Key to map numbers. These towns and cities appear in alphabetical order in the Gazetteer. Numbers in brackets show the number of pubs featured in each location.

1 Andover
2 Aston (Cheshire)
3 Banbury
4 Barmouth
5 Barton-upon-Humber
6 Beamish
7 Berkhamsted
8 Beverley
9 Birkenhead
10 Birmingham (3)
11 Blyth
12 Bourne End
13 Bradford on Avon
14 Bristol (4)
15 Broadstairs (3)
16 Burslem
17 Burton upon Trent
18 Bury St. Edmunds
19 Canvey Island
20 Carmarthen
21 Cauldon
22 Checkendon
23 Chester (3)
24 Cholmondeley
25 Claines
26 Claygate
27 Colnbrook
28 Combe Martin
29 Cresswell Quay
30 Defford
31 Drewsteignton
32 Dudley (4)
33 Dungeness

34 Edgehill
35 Edinburgh (4)
36 Bretforton
37 Exminster
38 Fancott
39 Faulkland
40 Gateshead
41 Geldeston
42 Glasgow
43 Guildford
44 Hallatrow
45 Harrogate
46 Havant
47 Herne
48 Herne Bay
49 Himley
50 Honey Street
51 Huish Episcopi
52 Ilfracombe
53 Kenfig
54 King's Nympton
55 Lacock
56 Leeds (3)
57 Liverpool
58 Llanthony
59 London (28)
  NB: Localities of individual pubs are in the index under 'London'
60 Lydiate
61 Manchester (4)
62 Margate
63 Napton
64 Newcastle upon Tyne (3)

65 Norton St Philip
66 Norwich
67 Nottingham (2)
68 Odcombe
69 Oxford
70 Peterborough
71 Piel Island
72 Pontfaen
73 Portishead
74 Portland
75 Ripley
76 Rosebush
77 Royston
78 St. Albans
79 St. Dogmaels
80 St. Mary Hoo
81 Sheerness-on-Sea
82 Sittingbourne
83 Sourton
84 South Shields
85 Stockport
86 Stockton (Warwickshire)
87 Sunderland
88 Swansea
89 Thame
90 Topsham
91 Tunbridge Wells
92 Wakefield (2)
93 Wallsend
94 Walsall
95 West Boldon
96 Wroxham
97 York (4)

2. GAZETTEER OF UNUSUAL PUBS

THE FOLLOWING PAGES contain a personal selection of Unusual Pubs listed alphabetically by city or town. All were open to customers at the time of publication. London has rather a lot of entries – the localities and featured pubs are listed in the main index. A map of locations appears opposite.

Information for walkers, cyclists and boat lovers is given beneath relevant entries under the headings 'by boot', 'by bike' or 'by boat'. General notes on these subjects start on page 137.

This is a subjective list of establishments which is not comprehensive – that would be a very large book. However, the author looks forward to receiving further suggestions from readers of pubs for inclusion in the next edition. Please use the dedicated Unusual Pubs Facebook page, www.fb.me/Unusualpubs, where updates on this book's content will also be posted, or write to him at bartonwrite1@gmail.com.

Notes

All establishments are licensed to sell alcohol. Where cask conditioned beer is available it is referred to as 'real ale'. ABV is Alcohol by Volume. NCN is National Cycle Network. Not all places sell meals and where they do it may be only on certain days or times. All information is given purely for guidance and may change at short notice.

Some establishments, particularly in rural areas, close in the afternoon or keep otherwise limited hours. Readers are strongly advised to check opening times before travelling.

Entries should not be considered recommendations in terms of drink, cuisine or service, the quality of which can be transient. Establishments stand on their own merit and have not paid or provided other inducements to be included.

'CAMRA' refers to the Campaign for Real Ale, an independent, consumer-run organization, founded in 1971 and committed to supporting Britain's unique beer style and pubs. For more details visit www.camra.org.uk, tel. 01727 867201.

ANDOVER, HAMPSHIRE

Working waterwheel – river runs through pub
The Town Mills, 20 Bridge Street, SP10 1BL.
Tel. 01264 332540. www.thetownmills.co.uk

This converted watermill, with its jumble of red-tiled roofs, is an unexpected sight in the town centre. Though a number of mills have been converted to pubs, this a rare one whose waterwheel still turns. Seated behind a glass partition, I was transfixed by its sight, sound and power. In 2013, customers helped raise £7000 to restore the derelict 8.5ft (2.59m) diameter wheel. The River Anton not only runs through the garden, fringed with reeds and a large weeping willow, but rushes through the pub itself, diving beneath customers' feet and the forecourt, then along a mill-race. Oak-beamed throughout, the downstairs bar has an atrium decorated with

The Town Mills, Andover, was built in 1764 and converted to a pub in 2001. A river runs through the building and turns a waterwheel inside.

Horses cool off in the River Anton, with the Town Mills, then still a functioning flour mill, in the background, c.1910.

survey of 1086. It was rebuilt in 1764 by millwright John Gibbs (as etched on a stone at the front) and continued milling grain until 1974. It had several incarnations as restaurant and night-club before its pub conversion in 2001. Ambient music; dog friendly.

By boot: A link to the River Anton Way, a 10-mile path to the Clatfords and River Test Way, via Rooksbury Mill, starts just south of the pub on Bridge Street. A shorter, circular walk is possible. *By bike:* NCN Route 246 crosses the town, linking with the Test Way to the south and going north to Kintbury, Berkshire to join NCN 4.

ASTON, CHESHIRE

A little bit of India – and beer Nirvana

The Bhurtpore Inn, Wrenbury Road, near Nantwich, CW5 8DQ. Tel. 01270 780917. www.bhurtpore.co.uk

The Siege of Bhurtpore in 1820s Rajasthan, India – a British victory commanded by Lord Combermere (a Cheshire estate owner) – led to the unique name. It was changed from the more prosaic Red Lion ten years later. That is the history lesson: the hostelry's present incarnation began in 1992 when Simon and Nicky George reopened the neglected pub and transformed it into a spacious, CAMRA award-winning place renowned for ale, food and hospitality. The Indian link is underlined with a selection of curries – a house speciality – and artefacts from the sub-continent. These include three tall wooden figures, one stationed behind the bar and festooned with clips from ales previously served. There are 11 hand-pumps and the real ale selection included the hoppy Deva Equinox (ABV 4.7%) and Three Tuns Clerics Cure IPA (5%) from Bishop's Castle, plus local Wrenbury Cider. 942 cask ales were served in 2015: current examples are detailed on a blackboard. The bottled beer list runs to 150 from around the world; spirits (notably whisky), food and wine menus are equally impressive. This is a drink connoisseur's dream come true. Regular meets of the Vintage

enamel signs, flour sacks and cart wheels, while upstairs is a lounge with sofas and a games room with pool tables and dartboard. There are many old photos and prints of the mill and its surroundings. Three Wadworth ales were on hand-pump, including 6X and rum-infused Swordfish (ABV 5%), which I accompanied with a roast from the Sunday carvery. A mill on this site was one of six recorded in Andover by the Domesday

A carved Indian figure stands, festooned with pump-clips, guarding the hand-pumps at the Bhurtpore Inn, Aston.

Ye Olde Reine Deer Inn, Banbury, showing the 'rescued' Globe Room today...

Japanese Motorcycle Club held. Garden; dog friendly.

By boot: The South Cheshire Way passes through the village and links with Wrenbury Station (one mile). **By bike:** On the Cheshire Cycleway (regional route 70). It offers a 176-mile circular ride.

BANBURY, OXFORDSHIRE

Oliver Cromwell's lost courtroom from the Civil War

Ye Olde Reine Deer Inn, Parsons Street, OX16 5NA.
Tel. 01295 270972. www.ye-olde-reinedeer-inn-banbury.co.uk

This former coaching inn, with its courtyard, oak beams, bare wooden floors and distinctive inn sign projecting over the street, has many tales from centuries past. Its most historic feature needs to be sought out. Walk through the main bar and along a narrow corridor, then climb three stone steps and you enter an elaborately panelled room with a big fireplace and

...and as depicted on a postcard sent in 1907, showing it being used as a courtroom by Parliamentarians during the Civil War.

paintings from the Civil War era. This is the Globe Room, named for a large globe of the world that once stood in the centre. It also had an ornate honeycomb plaster ceiling, though this was destroyed by a WWII bomb when it and the panelling was in storage, having been sold to a London antiques dealer in

1912. There was an outcry and the artefacts narrowly escaped export to the USA. The panels were rediscovered by experts from the Victoria & Albert Museum in the mid-1960s and reinstated in their original location by Banbury Council some sixteen years later. The room was used by Oliver Cromwell while he was laying siege to Banbury Castle and, it is claimed, for the Council of War that planned the Battle of Edge Hill. It was also used as a courtroom by the Parliamentarians, many Royalists being tried and sentenced within its confines. Real ales are from local brewer Hook Norton, and I particularly enjoyed the Mild. Meals are served lunchtime and evening. Garden; dog friendly.

By boot, bike and boat: The town is on the Oxford Canal, a good route for walkers, cyclists (NCN Route 5 Reading-Holyhead) and, of course, boaters. Tooley's Boatyard is cradle of the canal preservation movement. Mooring times vary according to zone; check information on towpath posts.

BARMOUTH, GWYNEDD

Indoor spring and rock pool
The Last Inn, Church Street, LL42 1EL.
Tel. 01341 280530. www.lastinn-barmouth.co.uk

Built into a mountainside opposite the harbour of this Victorian seaside resort, the pub is named after a cobblers' last – at its heart is a centuries-old shoemaker's cottage. Bare rock forms the inside rear wall and there is a large indoor pool. This is a natural feature, as is the spring that pours over the slate, constantly replenishing the crystal-clear pond. It even contains a healthy school of fish. The water-cooled grotto once doubled as a cellar, of sorts, being used to store beer casks. The local lifeboat crew is among the regulars: a RNLI flag decorates a wall signed by past and present members. This is a popular, candle-lit dining venue (booking advised) but there is a cosy bar area serving three real ales: Marston's Pedigree, Ringwood Boondoggle and Banks's Sunbeam. Outside seating at front; live music weekly.

The natural spring and rock pool inside Barmouth's Last Inn—once used in place of a cellar to cool the beer casks.

By boot: On the Wales Coast Path and Cambrian Way – the town is a good base for walking holidays. *By bike:* The 9½-mile Mawddach Trail to Dolgellau (also for walkers) starts here, crossing the estuary on a timber trestle bridge also carrying the coastal railway. The trail is traffic free and forms part of NCN Route 8 (Cardiff Bay-Holyhead). *By boat:* There is a seasonal passenger ferry across the estuary to Penrhyn Point (for Fairbourne).

BARTON-UPON-HUMBER, NORTH LINCOLNSHIRE

A Georgian windmill
The Old Mill, Market Lane, DN18 5DE.
Tel. 01652 660333 www.theoldmillbarton.com

For almost 150 years from 1803, it was busy grinding chalk and, later, milling barley to feed a malt kiln alongside.

The Old Mill at Barton-upon-Humber was a working windmill until 1950. During its conversion, a Saxon burial ground containing one hundred skeletons was unearthed.

Originally powered by six massive sails but, after one fell into the road, it was converted to run with an engine powered by coal gas. Production ceased in 1950 and the building stood idle, slowly disintegrating. Four decades later, it was re-born as a pub and restaurant and bought by brewers Marston's in 1993. The hostelry occupies much of the cavernous building but the highlight is walking into the base of the brick-built tower. There you can gaze upwards to see a maze of beams and the massive vertical shaft that once turned as it transferred power from the sails to the millstones. While enjoying your pint, it's easy to imagine the sound of creaking machinery and sacks of barley being winched to the top. During reconstruction, a Saxon burial ground containing more than a hundred skeletons was discovered on the site. Banks's Bitter and Wychwood Hobgoblin were on hand-pump on my visit and there was a varied food menu. Large garden.

By boot: The 148-mile Viking Way goes from Barton to **Oakham, Rutland, crossing the Lincolnshire Wolds and**

joining the Spa Trail. *By bike:* Barton is on NCN Route 1, the long distance East Coast route linking England and Scotland. It crosses the Humber Bridge to the north.

BEAMISH, CO. DURHAM

Rebuilt stone-by-stone and permanently set in 1913
The Sun Inn (formerly Tiger Inn), Beamish Museum, near Stanley, DH9 0RG. Tel. 0191 370 4000.
www.beamish.org.uk

The wind-up gramophone whirred into life with a music-hall favourite as a noisy tramcar rattled by outside. A fire was being teased into life in the grate and fresh sawdust was sprinkled on the wooden floor. I was witnessing another day beginning at this time-warp pub, permanently set in 1913. The stone-built Sun Inn and its decorative frontage was moved piece-by-piece from Bishop Auckland, where it was under threat of demolition, to the Beamish Living Museum of the North. Donated by Scottish and Newcastle Breweries, it began its new charmed life in 1985 and has since given thousands of visitors a taste of pre-Great War pub culture and decor in a cobbled street of period houses and shops that also open to visitors. Three local ales, brewed at Beamish Hall, are served on hand-pump (though sadly not at 1913 prices) and there are bottled beers from Consett Ale Works. The structure started life as a 'one up, one down' cottage built in the early 1800s. It became the Tiger Inn, was patronised by local miners and owned by the Leng family from 1857-99, before being taken over by James Deuchar's brewery (amalgamated with Newcastle Breweries in 1959). There is a public bar and a smaller snug or 'select room', complete with engraved glass and furnished with an ornate wooden bar counter and bar back, unusual fixed bench seating with fretwork and brass decoration, period fire surrounds and some attractive advertising mirrors from the museum's collection. There are some lovely period features such as a counter bell, a cast-iron match holder/striker in the shape of a

Moving experience: the Sun Inn at Beamish Museum was moved stone by stone from Bishop Auckland, where it was called the Tiger Inn. It has an immaculate period interior.

woodpecker, brass fittings and an assortment of stuffed animal heads. Pride of place is given to a taxidermied whippet, Jake's Bonny Mary, who won many racing trophies in his lifetime and was previously displayed in a pub called the Gerry near Tantobie, Co. Durham. The museum has exciting long-term plans, including opening an original Georgian coaching inn. Museum entrance charge payable.

By boot: A 3-mile circular Beamish Woods walk starts near the museum entrance. A map is available at www.thisisdurham.com. *By bike:* Long distance NCN Route 7 Sunderland-Inverness passes to the south. It forms two-thirds of the Sea to Sea (C2C) route, 35 miles of which is traffic free.

BERKHAMSTED, HERTFORDSHIRE

Front door is on canal not road – customers are advised 'nothing for you here'
The Rising Sun, Canal Side, George Street, HP4 2EG. Tel. 01442 864913. http://theriserberko.net

A board outside bears a photo of the Local Shop from BBC television's *League of Gentlemen* comedy and declares: 'There's nothing for you here.' A sign in the porch goes further: 'Everyone who passes through this door brings happiness. Some by entering and some by leaving.' Undeterred by quirky messages, people flock to 'the Riser', once a quiet Benskin's local, now a free house and community focal point. Contrary to its address, the pub is not on George Street, where a short alley leads to it. Instead, the entrance is on the Grand Union Canal towpath facing a lock, reflecting the waterway's past superiority as transport artery. Built in the 1880s and once incorporating stabling for canal horses, the layout is little changed. There's a compact, two-room bar with a separate snug (incorporating its own serving hatch). There are well trodden wooden floors, farmhouse chairs, benches and tables with peeling varnish, plus shelves of books and newspapers. I glanced up to see 17 framed CAMRA awards fixed to the ceiling, many for its success as a cider pub. There were 14 ciders on sale during my visit, along with five well chosen microbrewery ales, including Riser (ABV 3.7%) a quaffable house bitter from Tring Brewery. Havana cigars and tins of snuff are also available. 'We used to sell clay pipes, too,' said the barman, 'but there was little demand.' Dog owners are among the clientele, with free dog biscuits on the bar. As I noted this, one of the licensees returned from a walk with three large, grey Weimaraners. Notices advertised a wide range of events held at the pub. From regular cheese and folk clubs and monthly pop-up restaurant, to open-air theatre and a two-day Paint the Lock ('bring clothes you don't mind getting dirty'). As a 27-person choir struck up outside, the barman smiled knowingly and said 'We've got the morris dancers coming tomorrow, we'll have to get extra beer in.' Snacks; ambient music. Outside seating beside canal and covered patio.

By boot: The Grand Union Canal Walk was the first National Waterways Trail. It starts at London's Little Venice and uses the towpath to Birmingham. Locally, the Berkhamsted Waterways Walk is not one but three circular trails, from 2 to 6 miles in length, starting from the railway station – see www.chilternsaonb.org. *By bike:* The canal towpath provides good traffic-free cycling and Berkhamsted is on the Chilterns Cycleway, a 170-mile route through these uplands. *By boat:* Beside lock 55, with mooring nearby.

The Rising Sun in Berkhamsted faces a canal rather than a road, from where it attracts walkers, cyclists and boat crews eager to sample its quirky hospitality.

BEVERLEY, EAST YORKSHIRE

Unchanging tavern with gas lighting

White Horse (Nellie's), 22 Hengate, HU17 8BL. Tel. 01482 861973. www.nellies.co.uk (unofficial website).

Gas-lit, with a maze of stone-flagged and wood-floored parlours, scullery and other rooms, some with blazing coal fires and each filled with customers and the buzz of conversation. It was established as a coaching inn in the seventeenth century but is best-known for Nellie Collinson – whose family had the hostelry from 1927 and was licensee until the 1970s. Locals will tell you she is still there in spirit. It has been a Samuel Smith's house since the mid-1970s, with the Tadcaster brewery's good

The White Horse, Beverley has a maze of gas-lit rooms, with added illumination from candles on quiz nights.

value Old Brewery Bitter being poured at a rapid rate. The company's other beers are on keg. According to *Yorkshire's Real Heritage Pubs* (Ed. David Gamston, CAMRA Books 2011), the brewery introduced '... a bar-servery, whereas Nellie had made do with a simple table. Among many positives, though ... the old-fashioned front snug, second parlour and entrance corridors from Hengate were left gloriously untouched.' It is one of the author's favourite pubs and long may its quirkiness remain. A candle-lit quiz is held weekly. Outdoor seating in courtyard. Meals available at certain times.

By boot: Beverley is a town blessed with lovely architecture, long being relatively wealthy and a place of pilgrimage. Four town walking trails are based on the 39 medieval guilds of skilled workers once based here – from fletchers and hatters to jerkin makers and creelers (porters) – each depicted with a sculpture. See www.beverleytowntrail.co.uk. *By bike:* Situated on NCN Route 66 Manchester-Spurn Head via York.

BIRKENHEAD, MERSEYSIDE

Barber shop pub

Gallaghers, 20 Chester Street, CH41 5DQ.
Tel. 0151 649 9095. www.gallagherspubwirral.com

Who said men can't multi-task? In this pub they can enjoy a pint whilst having a haircut. There is a field of humour to mine here, with jokes about going home half-cut and sinking a pint beside the sink. It's welcoming for women too, being a rather cosy, family-run business. Gallaghers is half pub and half barbers' shop – the rear half, where two barbers' chairs rest on a tiled podium complete with mirrors, sink and a historical display of cut-throat and safety razors. The remainder of the pub is akin to a museum of military memorabilia, with items particularly relating to the Irish Guards (the landlord's previous career) and battleships, submarines and liners with a Merseyside link. Photographs, sailing ship models, uniforms, caps, crests –

The barber's shop section of Gallaghers, Birkenhead, where customers can enjoy a haircut whilst drinking real ale purchased from the bar in the background.

even regimental ice-buckets – are much in evidence. Many of the items were donated by customers.

It is the work of Frank and Suzanne Gallagher, both of whom are barbers and restored the pub from a derelict state in 2010. The building dates from the 1820s and features a glazed atrium above the bar, a decorative walnut bar counter, cast-iron columns and polished wooden floors. The landlords' efforts, including serving a changing variety of microbrewery ales, have been rewarded with numerous awards from CAMRA, including Merseyside Pub of the Year 2011. I enjoyed a hoppy pint of Brimstage Trapper's Hat (ABV 3.8%), brewed locally in the Wirral and a regular on the bar, which was lined with six hand-pumps. Other ales were from the Rat Brewery, Purple Moose, Salopian and Hawkshead on my visit. Food is served at certain times; barber's closed Sunday-Monday. There is a small garden laid with Astroturf and an upstairs bar used mainly by private parties. Ambient music; dogs welcome; no under eighteens.

By boot and bike: **Close to the 37-mile Wirral Circular Trail.** *By boat:* **Sail by 'Ferry 'cross the Mersey' from Liverpool to Birkenhead (the pub is five minutes' walk from the pier). Or take a Merseyrail train to Hamilton Square.**

BIRMINGHAM, WEST MIDLANDS

A palace of tiles

Bartons Arms, 144 High Street, Aston, B6 4UP.
Tel. 0121 333 5988. www.thebartonsarms.com

The beginning of the twentieth century is said to be the golden age of pub building. This Grade II* establishment, opened in 1901, is a veritable nugget. A display of Minton Hollins tiling fills almost every wall, vestibule and stairway with stunning

On the tiles: The Bartons Arms, Aston, is adorned with Minton Hollins tiling. Famous customers, from Laurel and Hardy and Charlie Chaplin to Ozzy Osbourne and Robert Plant, have used it.

colours. There are flower and leaf motifs in a palette including plum, turquoise, sea green and burnt umber; and a large hunting mural of equally vibrant ceramics. Other delights include ornate stained and engraved glass, wrought-iron stair balustrades and brass light fittings. Among extensive mahogany woodwork is an elaborate bar with revolving 'snob screens' (to preserve the privacy of Edwardian customers) in the former saloon. If any pub deserves the moniker of 'palace', it is this one. The three storey stone and brick neo-Jacobean building, with prominent gables and clock-tower, was designed by James & Lister Lea for brewer Mitchells & Butlers and their monogram features in some of the glasswork. After a prolonged closure, the pub was reopened in 2003 under the guardianship of Peterborough-based Oakham Ales: the four real ales served are from its range. Monthly tours can be booked, which incorporate a talk about its history, links to the lost Aston Hippodrome and a visit to the large cellar with its sloping floor and brick beer chute. (Visitors will also be shown this on request at quieter times.) A Thai restaurant occupies the former smoke room and the upstairs club and billiard rooms are used for meetings. Famous visitors have included Laurel and Hardy, Charlie Chaplin and, more recently, Ozzy Osbourne and Robert Plant. Ambient music; no outside seating.

By boot and bike: **A free Birmingham cycling and walking map is available from local libraries or see www.birmingham.gov.uk/cycling-map.**

A Tudor mansion

The Black Horse, Bristol Road South, Northfield, B31 2QT.
Tel. 0121 477 1800. www.jdwetherspoon.com

With its tall chimneys of Costwold stone, half-timbered walls and carved wooden details, you'd be excused for thinking this is a medieval manor house somehow transported from Shakespeare Country to a busy junction on the A38. In fact, the rambling structure was designed pre-WWII by Francis Goldsbrough and built in 1929-30 as the flagship pub for local brewer

The Black Horse, Northfield is an exquisite example of the inter-war pub style known as 'Brewers' Tudor'. The fantasy continues upstairs, where there is a reproduction baronial hall.

Davenports. It is probably the largest and most flamboyant example of a roadhouse in the inter-war style known as 'Brewers' Tudor', the reason for its rare Grade II* listing. It is a good example of a so-called 'improved' public house of the period, designed to reduce the anti-social behaviour associated with earlier urban hostelries. Close examination of the exterior reveals beautifully carved gargoyles and a Pegasus winged horse, along with a plethora of carved emblems. Along the projecting upper storey are rails decorated with carvings of folk quaffing ale and casks intertwined with hop garlands. Many windows have trefoil shapes and are inset with leaded glass. This drinkers' mansion was refurbished by the J.D. Wetherspoon chain in 2010 and sells a wide variety of real ales as well as the company's good-value food menu. Inside, the mock-Tudor theme continues. The ground floor boasts three ornate fireplaces, a barrel-vaulted and wood-panelled hallway, a conservatory and the Garden Room with its tie-beam roof. Upstairs, the fantasy continues with a reproduction baronial hall containing a large number of trefoil windows. A terraced garden, complete with bowls green, stone-

built clubhouse and horse sculpture fashioned from scrap metal, deserves inspection. It was originally intended to include formal gardens and no less than three pavilions but these were pruned from the original design. Nevertheless, one summer two female ducks found it appealing enough to lay their eggs there, hatching broods of ducklings which swam around paddling pools, to the amusement of customers and attracting media interest (*Birmingham Mail*, 4 July, 2014).

By boot and bike: Half-a-mile north-west of NCN Route 5 at Northfield Station. See also Bartons Arms entry.

Quirky and a brewery on the roof

The Lamp Tavern, 157 Barford Street, Highgate, B5 6AH. Tel. 0121 688 1220. http://stanwaybrewery.co.uk/lamp

This little gem is in an area of bland industrial lock-ups around Digbeth, ten minutes' walk from the city centre. A narrow bar is lined with upholstered bench seating and decorated with faded prints and photographs of a long vanished 'Brum.' The diminutive setting is invariably busy (with men only on my visits) and a fount of good conversation. It has been likened to sitting in someone's front room, with the long serving Eddie Fitzpatrick as affable 'mine host'. It is the only pub I have encountered with a microbrewery, Rock and Roll, situated on the roof. This was housed in a shed-like building, surrounded by roof tiles and chimneys, a visit to which involved negotiating a narrow staircase. Its popularity resulted in a move to larger premises in the Jewellery Quarter in summer 2016. The beers are still sold here, its spiritual home. Try Brew Springsteen (ABV 4%) or Instant Calmer (4.5%). Other good ales on the four hand-pumps included Everard's Tiger and the hard to find Stanway's, brewed in a Jacobean manor house. No meals but free snacks are often served. No ambient music; regular folk club in function room.

By boot: Inner-city Birmingham is not traditional walking territory but I have done several memorable pub crawls on foot around Digbeth. Make sure you include the

The Lamp Tavern had a microbrewery on the roof when this photo was taken in 2014. The brewing shed is just visible, on the right-hand lower roof.

Anchor and White Swan, both on CAMRA's National Inventory of historic interiors. *By bike*: See Bartons Arms entry.

BLYTH, NORTHUMBERLAND

1930s cinema with original projector
The Wallaw, 14 Union Street, NE24 2DX.
Tel. 01670 356830. www.jdwetherspoon.co.uk

Highly commended by CAMRA and English Heritage in the Pub Design Awards 2015, this 1930s cinema was converted to a pub for J.D. Wetherspoon, opening in 2013. The cavernous brick building in the Moderne style opened as the 1400-seat Wallaw (named after its owner Walter Lawson) in November 1937. Ant and Dec, Ken Dodd and Freddie Starr all appeared here but, after several changes of ownership, it closed in 2004 and lay dormant until its current revival. The foyer is breathtaking, complete with sweeping staircases that now lead only to the ladies toilet, gilt decoration, deco-style 'lady' lamps and the original Westar 'Peerless' projector. Now mounted on a stone plinth, this was discovered abandoned in the projection room. The auditorium is largely intact, complete with the seats in the upstairs circle (unlike The Ritz, Wallsend, q.v.). A bar counter runs the length of the former stage, and the screen has been obscured by a 'Sun Ray' mirrored façade. The attention to detail by the conversion architects is admirable. In addition to the statuette lamps already mentioned, there is a period clock and ceramic fire surround, 1930s-style signage, illuminated uplighters and canvas artworks saluting the silent film era. (The Wallaw stands on the site of William Tudour's Hippodrome which introduced moving pictures to Blyth.) There are ten hand-pumps with a wide selection of guest ales. I enjoyed a malty pint of Young Henry's (ABV 4.0%) and there is an all-day menu. Outside seating on roadside patio.

By bike: **Blyth is situated on the North Sea Cycle Route, NCN 1 – claimed to be the world's longest cycle route.**

The foyer of the Wallaw, Blyth, a former cinema transformed by J.D. Wetherspoon in 2013, showing the original Westar 'Peerless' projector.

BOURNE END, BUCKINGHAMSHIRE

Only accessible on foot or by boat
The Bounty, SL8 5RG. Tel: 01628 520056.
http://thebountypub.com

I first encountered the Bounty, on its water meadow beside the River Thames, while on a boating holiday. Being able to moor beside its garden and order a pint from a bar counter resembling the prow of a boat was a hoot. I didn't know then that this was the only way to reach it, unless you were walking the Thames Path, which passes its door. No public roads go near, so 'petrol heads' are out of luck. A sign above the door announces that this is 'The People's Republic of Cock Marsh'. It's a joke of course, though the marsh is extraordinary. Belonging to the National Trust, it is a Site of Special Scientific Interest and includes burial mounds thought to date from the early Bronze Age. For a time, it also boasted a landing strip for light aircraft – once used by aviation pioneer Amy Johnson. The pub stands on the site of the Quarry Hotel, built to cater for Victorian pleasure-seekers and destroyed by fire in 1938. Busy with dog-walkers, families and hikers during summer weekends, the place becomes a haven of peace between October and March, when it is open until dusk at weekends only. The large main bar, with its boat-shaped counter, is decorated with international flags, yachting pendants and other assorted memorabilia. It doubles as a sweet shop, serving confectionery, ice-cream and greetings cards, while sport fans can avail themselves of a dartboard and billiard table. The rear room is laid out for diners and this has a view across Cock Marsh, along with a display of local historical photographs (including the flood of January 2003 when the pub was marooned) and second-hand books for sale. Three ales were available on a recent visit: two from the local Rebellion Brewery (Mutiny and IPA, rebadged as house beer) plus a guest, Andwell Touchold Engage, and Old Rosie Cider. There is outdoor seating facing the river and a play area for children. Meals served (Sunday lunch only in winter). Dog friendly; ambient music.

By foot: On the long distance Thames Path and ten minutes' walk from Bourne End Station (where there is car parking), via a walkway attached to the railway bridge across the river. *By boat:* Those with a boat can moor outside, otherwise there are occasional steamboat pleasure trips operated by Thames Steamers from Bourne End Marina (which also necessitates walking to the pub by the above route).

Though the Bounty at Bourne End cannot be reached by car, this has not deterred a crowd of customers, who have found their way to the Thames-side pub by boat or on foot. A sign tells them they have arrived at 'The People's Republic of Cock Marsh.'

BRADFORD-ON-AVON, WILTSHIRE

A tug-boat snug
The Lock Inn Café, Frome Road, BA15 1LE.
Tel. 01225 868068. www.thelockinn.co.uk

This pub-café, seemingly straight out of *Swallows and Amazons*, serves two draught real ales, scrumpy cider and other alcoholic drinks, plus meals all day. A tree-shaded haven beside the

A narrowboat glides past Fat Dickie's Tug, a floating snug at the Lock Inn beside the Kennet and Avon Canal, Bradford-on-Avon. The pub-café, and its three summer houses, are hidden behind willows.

Kennet and Avon Canal, it offers a variety of drinking spaces – three summer-houses, a quayside and a boat – as well as the stone-built cottage with quarry-tiled floors. As well as a small bar counter, the latter is packed with a diverse collection of memorabilia, including a phonograph, typewriter, a factory clocking-on machine, assorted lamps and examples of 'Roses and Castles' canal hardware. Cream teas and the boatman's breakfast are popular. Fat Dickie's Tug, permanently moored alongside, is a converted narrowboat with drinking areas at each end, decorated with flower baskets and a nautical bell. Ales served on my visit were Kennet and Avon Rusty Lane and St Austell Tribute. Bicycles and canoes for towpath and canal exploration can be rented next door. Dog friendly.

By boot, boat and bike: Situated beside bridge 172 on the Kennet and Avon Canal and towpath and NCN Route 4, which link the Avon at Bath with the Thames at Reading. Adjacent to the town wharf.

BRETFORTON, WORCESTERSHIRE

Witches' circles keep out evil spirits

The Fleece Inn, The Cross, near Evesham, WR11 7JE.
Tel. 01386 831173. www.thefleeceinn.co.uk

Beginning as a medieval longhouse, the Fleece has a remarkable pedigree, its present incarnation being a seventeenth-century timber-framed building. There's a warren of rooms with oak beams, flagstone floors and creaky wooden settles. Situated beside a stone cross and surrounded by hollyhocks, it is the focal point of this pretty village in the Vale of Evesham. In fine weather, drinkers also relax in a spacious apple orchard. The inn was owned by generations of the same family—the last being Lola Taplin, who lived there all her life. On her death, aged seventy-seven in 1977, she bequeathed it to the National Trust. A fire in 2004 could have marked its death-knell; instead it has been lovingly restored and you would never guess a flame burned

The Pewter Room in the Fleece Inn, Bretforton, showing three witches' circles in front of the hearth. The fireback is embossed with the year 1670.

in anger. In accordance with Lola's wishes, a medieval tradition of witches' circles is maintained. Painted or chalked in white, in front of each fireplace, they are said to trap evil spirits attempting to enter via the chimney. It is not certain when the superstition began but they have been drawn so often that there are circular indentations in the stone floor. Circles, to concentrate or contain 'energy', are seen in several branches of witchcraft but it is believed that these are the only surviving examples in an English inn. There is a display of 300 year-old pewter.

Up to five ales are served, including Uley Pig's Ear and Wye Valley Bitter, along with real ciders (try the house Ark – ABV 6%). Meals are served, booking is advised. There is regular folk music, Morris dancing and other events, including a January Wassail and summer Asparagus Festival. On CAMRA's National Inventory; dog friendly; outdoor seating.

By boot: Different footpaths link the pub to Honeybourne railway station and the Cotswold Way National Trail (at Broadway, 4 miles south). By bike: The eastern section of NCN Route 442 to Hanborough starts at Honeybourne (2½ miles via local roads).

BRISTOL

Theatre and art gallery

The Alma Tavern & Theatre, 18-20 Alma Vale Road, Clifton, BS8 2HY. Tel. 0117 973 5171.
www.almatavernandtheatre.co.uk

This Victorian hostelry in the centre of Clifton not only contains the city's oldest pub theatre, it also has an informal gallery of locally produced art in the rear bar. Everything is for sale, sold commission free to support artists. The compact theatre is upstairs, converted from two function rooms in 1997, containing 40 seats in tiered rows. It features a programme of amateur and professional productions. These range from shows for children as young as four to adult comedy and drama by

The author enjoys a beer during a lull in rehearsals at Bristol's Alma Tavern, the city's oldest pub-theatre.

aspiring new writers. In 2016, the venue's first Shakespearean Summer School was held for young actors. Downstairs, there are two bars sharing a large central servery. Polished wooden floors and restrained decor create a stylish but informal atmosphere. Three ales were being served, Bath Gem, St Austell Tribute and Sharp's Doom Bar, plus food available all day. Regular live music. Outdoor seating on patio; ambient music.

By boot and bike: The city is seen to good advantage on foot, especially around the harbour area. A series of city walking routes and cycling information can be viewed at http://travelwest.info/walk. Greater Bristol was the first UK Cycling City and Cyclebag, the forerunner of Sustrans, began here in the 1970s. A pioneering project was the conversion of a Bristol to Bath track-bed to a cycle path, still a popular route.

Paraphernalia, pets and pump-clips

Cornubia, 142 Temple Street, BS1 6EN.
Tel. 0117 925 4415. http://thecornubia.co.uk

Tucked away off a main thoroughfare, it started life as a Georgian wig-maker's shop but is now home to a hair-raising collection of objects and animals. There are hundreds of pump clips, of ales once served on the premises, that festoon ceilings, walls and other surfaces. These compete with flags from across the British Isles, draped across the main ceiling and around the bar counter. Horse brasses and military paraphernalia rub shoulders with shelves of books and board games with names like Mid-Life Crisis and Downfall. The main attraction for me, however, was the menagerie of pets. Namely, tanks of tropical fish and terrapins, along with dogs and a boisterous parrot. 'We take him upstairs each evening as he can get over-excited,' advises the barman. 'He has escaped a few times and takes pleasure in dive-bombing the customers.' Completing this dazzling array of decor are Tiffany lamps and garlands of fairy lights. It boasts an excellent selection

A tank of terrapins and a parrot's cage – just part of the pub's menagerie – can be seen in this view of Cornubia. The Bristol pub was variously a wig-maker's shop and home to the Hidden Brewery.

of real ale – this was once home to the Hidden Brewery. By the Horns, Springhead and Outstanding were among the brewers represented on my visit. The 'L' shaped interior is compact and cosy. Ambient music: a sound-track of 'oldies' from the likes of Roy Orbison, Led Zeppelin and the Kinks. Snacks including pork pies, pasties and pickled eggs. Outside seating at the front and in a secluded beer garden. Dog friendly.

By boot and bike: See page 30.

Barge that once carried grain now sells ale made with it

The Grain Barge, Mardyke Wharf, Hotwell Road, Hotwells, BS8 4RU Tel. 0117 929 9347. www.grainbarge.co.uk

Built in the city's shipyards in 1936, this spacious cargo vessel started life as an engineless craft that was towed by tug, with cargoes of wheat and barley, hence the name. It was born again

Ale sail: The Grain Barge, moored in Bristol's floating harbour, sells a range of Bristol Beer Factory ales and is a popular live music venue.

as a floating bar and restaurant seventy years later, with recycled materials used in the re-fit. Though it no longer sails, the barge offers those who come aboard splendid maritime views across the floating harbour, including of Brunel's *SS Great Britain*, moored opposite. It is part of the Bristol Beer Factory set-up, selling a range of the company's highly regarded ales (I had the hoppy Nova at ABV 3.8%) as well as other microbrewery guests, on five hand-pumps. There are three decks: the top one being open-air, while below is the main bar – wood-floored with large picture windows. The hold is reserved for regular live music. My visit was before a 2016 refurbishment which included additional seating and other improvements.

By boot: The harbour area is ideal for walkers, being well signposted and including information points which show key points of interest and street maps (see also page 30). By boat: Yellow water taxis serve the harbour area. The barge's 2016 makeover included a new landing station, allowing customers to arrive directly by water.

Victorian tramcar snug

King's Head, 60 Victoria Street, BS1 6DE. Tel. 0117 929 2338.

From the outside, this hostelry near Temple Meads Station seems unremarkable, though the building is seventeenth century. Inside is a feast of polished wood and decorative glass and the pub is deservedly on CAMRA's National Inventory of historic interiors. Many of the sumptuous fittings along the long, narrow bar date from *circa* 1865, notably a bar-back with a series of arches advertising popular drinks of the period. Towards the rear is a unique feature added later in the Victorian era: the Tramcar Bar snug. So-called because its curved and part glazed wooden panels, door and bench seating resemble an old tram. To sit inside is to take a Dickensian excursion. Hold tight! Topping one of the panels is another surviving treasure, an ornate cigar lighter, once gas powered, while bell pushes remain from the days of waiter service. There are photos and

Polished wood panelling, and a low door (open, in foreground) form the Tramcar Bar in the King's Head, Bristol. Fittings include bell-pushes once used for waiter service and a cigar lighter, fixed above the right-hand panel.

prints of veteran trams and city scenes. Four hand-pumps were dispensing ales from Skinner's, Otter, Sharp's and Fuller's, while the lunchtime menu included 'flat hats': large Yorkshire puddings with a choice of fillings.

By boot and bike: See page 30.

BROADSTAIRS, KENT

Castle folly on cliff-top

Captain Digby, Whiteness Road, Kingsgate, CT10 3QH. Tel. 01843 867764. www.captaindigby.co.uk

Stone-built, fortress-like and perched on the edge of chalk cliffs, it makes a stunning sight overlooking Kingsgate Bay. There has been a hostelry on the site since the eighteenth century, when

the eccentric Lord Holland (owner of the sprawling mansion nearby, Holland House) built a combined folly and inn for his guests. He named it in honour of his nephew, naval hero Captain Robert Digby. The original building fell into the sea during storms over the years. The oldest part seen today dates from *circa* 1816, with extensions added in the 1970s. Beneath the floor is a large cavern which was reputedly used by notorious local smugglers, the Snelling gang. Until a few years

Period postcard showing the Captain Digby, built as an 'entertainment venue' by Lord Holland. There is a cavern, possibly once used by smugglers, in the cliffs below.

The Captain Digby today, showing its dramatic cliff-top location between Margate and Broadstairs.

ago it was possible to get to the beach via a trap-door in the cellar. This cavernous, all-day dining pub is popular with families (play areas for children). There were two ales on when I visited, the local Gadd's No.7 and Sharp's Doom Bar. Garden.

By boot and bike: **The Viking Coastal Trail (NCN regional Route 15) passes the pub en route between Broadstairs and Margate (q.v.).**

Former chapel doubles as a bookshop

The Chapel, 44-46 Albion Street, CT9 1EU.
Tel. 07837 024259.

Situated in the old part of this maritime town is a hostelry every bit as characterful as the sea-dogs who used to live hereabouts. It occupies part of former St Mary's Chapel, dating from 1601, though the site is much older. It once contained a famous shrine

Customers using the Chapel, Broadstairs, are surrounded by thousands of second-hand books. The bar frontage resembles an altar screen, while hymn and psalm numbers are posted on boards for a non-existent congregation.

venerated by mariners. For the last few decades it has been a second-hand bookshop. Many pubs have small libraries but this one is huge, covering two floors and several rooms, lined with thousands of volumes for sale. It offers a perfect diversion for solitary drinkers, and those whose drinking companions become tiresome: just pick up a book. The ecclesiastical past is recalled with an ornate bar frontage resembling a carved altar screen; hymn and psalm numbers are displayed for a departed congregation; and candles burn in tall brass candlesticks. There is a wood-burning stove for cooler days, and money is deposited in an old-fashioned cash register. Ale is drawn straight from the cask with the stillage directly behind the bar. Three tasty local brews were available on my visit (from Tonbridge, Westerham and Finchcock's breweries) along with cider, perry, mead and Kentish wine. The food is locally sourced too, specialities being pie and mash, cheese and shellfish, with local crab and lobster often available. There is ambient music plus regular live music. One regret: I was so busy chatting to fellow customers and sampling the beers that I didn't have time to browse the books.

By boot and bike: **Close to the Viking Coastal trail (NCN regional Route 15), a 32-mile circuit of the Isle of Thanet, including Margate (q.v.) and Ramsgate. There is a historical walking trail of Broadstairs available from tourist offices and downloadable from the Internet.**

Nineteenth-century stable

Yard of Ale, 61 Church Street, St Peter-in-Thanet,
CT10 2TU. Tel. 07790 730205.

This cosy den could be straight out of Laurie Lee's *Cider With Rosie*. Sitting on a bale of hay in the sawdust-strewn stable, supping a pint of ale or cider drawn from the cask, is a rustic pleasure possible here. Other furnishings in the brick-and-rubble building, with its cobbled floor, include bench seating, stools and narrow tables fixed between the former horse bays. A solid fuel stove provides heat in winter. Decorated with garlands of hops and rows of pump clips, along with leather

The Yard of Ale is a former stable, its horse-bays still intact and with seating including bales of straw. Beer and cider comes straight from the cask.

horse tackle, farmyard tools and other oddments. There is no bar as such, but a part glazed bay at one end where drinks are dispensed. The limited space encourages friendly banter and I found the locals keen to tell me about the area's highlights – and other nearby drinkers' delights, such as the Four Candles brewpub, also in the village. A covered outdoor area in the stable yard contains picnic-style benches and you can examine a horse trough and, bizarrely, a gravestone marked Elizabeth Noble (the pub is adjacent to a funeral directors). Chalk boards indicated five ciders and four ales available, with Naylors, Burning Sky, Bradfield and Mighty Oak the breweries represented when I visited. Simple pubs snacks such as pork pies, pickled eggs and pork scratchings. The 'nose bag' menu helpfully indicated that 'handfuls of hay are provided free.' The only thing missing from this gem are the horses: I half expected

one to trot in and be offered a pint. Winner of several local and regional CAMRA awards, including finalist for National Pub of the Year 2015. Dog friendly.

By bike: This, and the other Broadstairs and Margate pubs featured, are within a few miles of each other. A ride combining them, including part of the Viking Trail along the coast (see previous entry) is easy and enjoyable.

BURSLEM, STAFFORDSHIRE

Hidden hotel
The Leopard, 21 Market Place, near Stoke-on-Trent, ST6 3AA. Tel. 01782 819644.

This three-storey hotel, opposite the town hall, was once the 'Savoy of the Midlands' but it closed in the early 1950s. The rooms were sealed off with their memories and, reputedly, ghosts. It has, however, continued as a pub. Sharon, one of the licensees, unlocked an anonymous door and led my friends and me by

One of the hidden hotel corridors of the 'Savoy of the Midlands', closed off and reputedly haunted, behind the Leopard pub, Burslem, since the 1950s.

torchlight through dark corridors lined with 55 empty bedrooms. Paint and wallpaper is peeling, bare floorboards creaked and shafts of daylight danced like fireflies on aging varnished woodwork. In its day, Ava Gardner and Laurel and Hardy were among the clientele. Now the only 'guests' in this hidden labyrinth are participants in regular ghost tours. Novelist Arnold Bennett wrote about the place, calling it the Leopard. In 1765, Josiah Wedgwood and James Brindley dined while discussing the building of the Trent and Mersey Canal, a significant episode of the Industrial Revolution. There's a tiled entrance and the public rooms hint towards the opulent past, with upholstered bench seating and mahogany panels decorated with leaded and coloured glass (even the entrance to the gents' is ornate). The ballroom now hosts live bands instead of soirees, but a tunnel from the cellar to the town hall is sealed. Five real ales were available, including two from Cottage; Bass and Coach House Toffee Bitter are the regulars. Meals served some evenings and Sunday lunchtimes (booking advised). Ambient music, garden. Tours of the hotel, including ghost tours, are by arrangement.

By boot and boat: **Half-a-mile east of the Trent and Mersey Canal between Stoke and Middleport.** *By bike:* **A short distance west of NCN Route 5 (Reading-Holyhead) where it crosses the B5051.**

The hallowed back room of the Coopers Tavern, Burton upon Trent, in 2008. Adjacent to the Bass Brewery, it was the fiefdom of senior staff until the 1950s.

BURTON UPON TRENT, STAFFORDSHIRE

No bar counter; once 'personal pub' of Bass brewers

Coopers Tavern, 43 Cross Street, DE14 1EG.
Tel. 01283 532551. www.cooperstavern.co.uk

Burton was England's brewing 'capital' for many years and this sturdy, detached house near the town centre is the former Bass brewery tap. By 1826 it was a store for the company's Imperial Stout but later had a more important role, according to pub historian Geoff Brandwood. 'It had attractions for senior members of the brewery, who used it as a kind of personal pub ... the back area remained the fiefdom of the selected few until about 1950: the hoi polloi were served at a hatch door.' (*Britain's Best Real Heritage Pubs*, CAMRA, 2013, 140). There are three rooms, including a snug but no conventional bar counter. At least one ale (usually Bass) is served directly from the cask, with Joule's Ales on hand-pump and several real ciders. With beer memorabilia around the walls and varnished bench seating, this still has the feel of an 'inner sanctum' that I felt privileged to enjoy. Listed on CAMRA's National Inventory of historic interiors and holder of several CAMRA pub and cider awards. Regular folk music; snacks, such as pork pies, are usually available. Dog friendly; small garden.

By boot: **A 10½-mile circular walk goes down the Trent and Mersey Canal and returns via the River Trent. See the website www.centralrivers.org.uk.** *By bike:* **Burton is on NCN Route 54 between Lichfield and Derby, while NCN 63 links the town with Wisbech via Leicester. Sections of the canal towpath are good for cycling.** *By boat:* **A short walk east of bridge 33 (Shobnall Road) on the Trent and Mersey Canal.**

BURY ST. EDMUNDS, SUFFOLK

'Smallest pub' – and a mummified cat

The Nutshell, The Traverse, IP33 1BJ.
Tel. 01284 764867. www.thenutshellpub.co.uk

Author: 'Do you have a mummified cat in here?' Barman: 'What, like the one hanging above your head?' Author: Is it alright to take photographs?' Barman: 'Yes as long as they're not attached to the wall.' Even without a joking barman, the Nutshell is a remarkable pub. The oldest surviving claimant to the title of England's smallest pub, its dimensions are a mere 15ft by 7ft (or for lovers of the metric system, eight square metres). Hardly room to swing a cat; I have been in bigger bathrooms. It also merits a place on CAMRA's National Inventory of historic interiors. A bare-boards hostelry, whose humble beginnings were as a simple beerhouse *circa* 1867, its central location is opposite a spacious Wetherspoon's in the old

In a Nutshell: 'the country's smallest pub', in Bury St. Edmunds, was once famous for its museum of strange artefacts. A mummified cat can still be seen.

Corn Exchange. The hostelry is crammed with artefacts that, aside from the above cat, which was found walled up in a nearby building, include a stag's head, vintage cigarette packets and a stuffed rabbit. These appear to be a nod to a 'museum of curiosities' started by a Victorian landlord, John Stebbing. The ceiling is lined with currency notes, mainly foreign, as are the coins decorating the walls. I found the place almost full with about a dozen people, though the record is said to be 102 and a dog named Blob. The atmosphere was remarkably friendly and included a local man who appeared to have an encyclopaedic knowledge of the pub. There is an historical display upstairs, reached by climbing a narrow flight of stairs. Two ales by the town's brewer Greene King were on sale, Abbot and IPA. The nearby brewery has an interesting visitor centre. No meals.

By boot: **The St Edmund Way is a 79-mile walk through Suffolk via Bury, from Manningtree, Essex to Brandon, Norfolk.** *By bike:* **NCN Route 13, running north/south and 51, going east/west, meet in town.**

CANVEY ISLAND, ESSEX

Situated below sea level – and inspiration to Charles Dickens

The Lobster Smack, Haven Road, SS8 0NR.
Tel. 01268 514297. www.thelobstersmackcanveyisland.co.uk

Dark clouds were billowing above a slate grey Thames Estuary and attendant salt-marshes as fierce gusts of wind tried to topple me off the sea wall. I was balancing on this, attempting to photograph the pub, known in the 1700s as The World's End. Outwardly at least, with its weather-boarding and leaded bottle windows, it has changed little since the bleak location lent inspiration to author Charles Dickens. In *Great Expectations* he calls it the Ship Inn. From this hideout Pip rows convict Magwitch out to meet a paddle-steamer that would take him to freedom, only to be thwarted by police and a fellow convict, Compeyson. Today, adjacent chalet homes and an oil storage depot have changed the surroundings dramatically. There are some lovely old local photos, however, in this former Seabrookes Brewery pub. Its wood beamed interior has had a modern makeover and is divided between a restaurant and more informal bar area. Upstairs, there is a more rustic feel to the Drifters Bar, popular with locals on my visit and reached via an entrance beside the sea wall. Pool and darts is played. Both bars have a selection of real ales: Adnams Broadside and Ghost Ship,

This postcard, stamped in 1924, clearly shows the Lobster Smack's situation below sea level. The Canvey Island inn inspired Charles Dickens for a scene in Great Expectations.

The same view of the Lobster Smack, in 2015. Apart from the reinforced sea wall, the scene has changed remarkably little.

Sharp's Doom Bar and Greene King IPA on my visit. Food is served all day; a wide-ranging menu which included mussels in garlic sauce. There is a large garden and front patio area. Canvey is protected from flooding by miles of sea wall and a system of sluices. The pub, too, is below sea level and similarly protected. It was almost certainly a haunt for smugglers and a row of former preventive men's (coastguard) cottages can be seen nearby. It was also renowned for illegal boxing matches, held for many years in what is now the car park. Ambient music, occasional live music; dog friendly.

By boot: A footpath follows the perimeter of the island and, from Benfleet Station, the distance to the pub is approximately 7 miles (less than 3 by road). *By boat:* Those with their own vessel can moor at nearby Hole Haven.

CARMARTHEN, CARMARTHENSHIRE

Possibly Wales' smallest pub – and a shrine to rugby
The Plume of Feathers, St Mary's Street, SA31 1TN.
Tel. 01267 222151.

If this three-storey Brains pub, in a narrow lane near the castle, is not the smallest pub in Wales it is certainly the most compact. It crams a wide selection of rugby memorabilia and photographs, along with a dartboard, wood-slatted bar counter and some fixed bench seating into its diminutive two-room layout. Any more than ten customers makes the place seem full. A serving hatch over the stairs allows staff to serve customers unable to reach the bar on busy days; while a trap-door in the floor enables beer casks to be dropped into the cellar. Two narrow staircases, one up to private rooms, the other down to the toilets, are squeezed between the two rooms. The actors – and noted drinking companions – Richard Burton, Oliver Reed and Richard Harris patronized the pub when filming *Under Milk Wood* in Laugharne, 13 miles distant. On CAMRA's National Inventory of historic interiors. Ambient music, no food.

Carmarthen's Plume of Feathers is so small getting a drink can be difficult. This shows the serving hatch by the stairs, used by customers unable to reach the bar on busy days.

By boot: Carmarthen is situated on the 870-mile Wales Coast Path, a continuous walk around Wales. The section from Ferryside follows the course of the Afon Tywi into the centre of town. *By bike:* On the Celtic Trail, long distance NCN Route 4 (London-Fishguard).

CAULDON, STAFFORDSHIRE

Quirky museum of bygones
The Yew Tree Inn, ST10 3EJ. Tel. 01538 309876.
www.yewtreeinncauldon.com

'The yew tree outside is older than the pub – and that's four hundred years old,' says Alan East, mine host for the past fifty-five years (though he now shares the role with his stepson). Everything has a long pedigree here, not least the wondrous collection of objects that fills this rambling, oak-beamed hostelry. There is an assortment of polyphons, the Victorian equivalent of juke-boxes, some resembling grandfather clocks and many working when you drop in a two-pence coin. There are also pianolas, symphonions, assorted wirelesses and miners' lamps, rifles and a bizarre wind instrument called 'the serpent'. Musician Roy Wood, who lives locally, once had a go. Money is deposited in an ornate brass cash register unchanged since the days of pounds, shillings and pence. Among the other memorabilia are penny farthing bicycles, a pair of Queen Victoria's silk stockings and the rather inhumane 'Acme Dog Carrier' (a joke). You can have a go at table skittles, darts or dominoes, bring an instrument to fortnightly jam sessions or join with the 'Cauldon Philosophical and Debating Society' at the bar each evening. Seating is an assortment of church pews, benches and settles. As you may surmise, a sense of humour is a requirement here and the staff are full of bonhomie. The Yew Tree's location is remote – in the Staffordshire Peak District between Leek and Ashbourne – with the tall chimney of a nearby cement works acting as a landmark. There were three ales available when I visited: Burton Bridge Bitter, Rudgate

Antique clocks and rifles are among the items adorning the bar of the Yew Tree Inn, Cauldon. One of the pub's collection of working polyphons – the Victorian equivalent of a juke-box – is seen in the foreground.

Ruby Mild, Cottage Brewing Duchess, plus Slack Alice Cider. Food includes Staffordshire pies, pasties and oatcakes. Winner of several CAMRA awards. Dog friendly; seating in stable yard and garden.

By boot and bike: **A mile from Waterhouses on the traffic-free Manifold Track of the former Leek & Manifold Light Railway. NCN Route 54 links with other Peak District trails.** *By boat:* **4½ miles from Froghall Basin on the Caldon Canal.**

CHECKENDON, OXFORDSHIRE

Rustic house in a woodland clearing

Black Horse, Burncote Lane, Scots Common, RG8 0TE.
Tel. 01491 680418.

Red kites were gliding overhead and horses grazing as I cycled towards this pub, eager for a break from my perambulations in the Chiltern Hills. Aside from a couple of barns and stables, it is isolated in a woodland clearing. At first glance, the low

A customer relaxes on the veranda of the Black Horse, Checkendon. The isolated, time-warp pub was purchased for £30 in 1905.

building is all roof tiles and veranda. Deeds on display show the homestead was bought in 1905 for the princely sum of £30 by ancestors of the family that still runs it. It has hardly changed in the intervening eleven decades. Decor is horse brasses and flat irons and the quarry tiled bar has a low, sagging ceiling, so mind your head. There are two further rooms with brick fireplaces and furniture reminiscent of the 1950s, linked by a narrow corridor. Taking my order, the barman disappeared into an adjacent room to pour the ale – selected from two brews by West Berkshire and one from Marlow's Rebellion – from the cask. The bar was busy with locals, walkers and horse riders and the conversation was lively. There was no competing piped music, television or other modern distractions. Toilets are outside and the lean-to gents' puts a new slant on the word 'basic.' Outdoor benches under the veranda and in garden. Simple bar snacks; no meals or credit cards. Dog friendly. Opening hours vary in winter.

By boot and bike: **The Chilterns Area of Outstanding Natural Beauty has a wide range of walking and cycling routes. A good starting point for planning is the website www.chilternsaonb.org.**

CHESTER, CHESHIRE

World War I memorials

Albion Inn, Park Street, CH1 1RN. Tel: 01244 340345.
www.albioninnchester.co.uk

'Thomas Hopley, killed in action, Arras, March 1918'; 'James Henry Ward, killed by shell explosion in France, October 1916.' Four brass plaques to lost soldiers, officially recognized by the War Memorials Trust and adorned with poppies, are secured to the walls of this immaculate pub. Dating from the 1880s, it stands, complete with engraved glass in sash windows, at the end of a Victorian terrace near the city walls. The Great War is remembered everywhere: through period cartoons, photographs,

We shall remember them: one of the official World War I memorials in Chester's Albion Inn. The pub is filled with reminders of the Great War.

Medieval Great Hall

The Brewery Tap, Gamul House, 52-54 Lower Bridge Street, CH1 1RU. Tel: 01244 340999. www.the-tap.co.uk

King Charles I could have done with a few pints of Spitting Feathers the night he stayed here: the following day his army was defeated at the Battle of Rowton Moor (1645). The late medieval Great Hall was then home to the influential Gamull family, and the first floor entrance indicates it once had an elevated walkway of the type found today on the city's well-known Rows. Spitting Feathers is a local brewery (based, coincidentally, adjacent to the battle site) that owns this impressive pub. A Classical doorway leads to the huge hall, dating from the early 1500s, hung with tapestries and open to the roof, as it would have been originally. There are elliptical windows, rough oak beams and a large carved stone fireplace. Part of one original wall has been left to reveal its wooden construction, including mud and manure render. A long bar counter is lined with eight hand-pumps and, as well as the

posters, sheet music and military rifles. The menu, described as 'trench rations,' includes corned beef hash, haggis and Staffordshire oatcakes. The only things missing are anti-macassars on the chairs and squaddies having a sing-song around the pianola (there is one). Enamel signs advertise Colman's Wash Blue, Virol malt extract and Craven 'A' cigarettes, while a coal fire blazes in the snug, one of the three rooms, fringed with a beautiful cast-iron and tile fireplace. A centrally positioned bar counter is covered with more period advertising, while one in the corner room features magic lanterns. Two real ales were available, Moorhouses Pride of Pendle and Bombardier Gold. Dog friendly. Accommodation available.

By boot: Chester City Walls Trail forms a 2-mile circuit around the centre; the Millennium Trail links 40 heritage buildings; while the Shropshire Union Canal provides 15 miles of walking between Waverton and Ellesmere Port. *By bike:* NCN Route 5 (Reading-Holyhead) and NCN Route 45 (Chester-Salisbury) are among trails converging here. The Shropshire Union towpath can also be cycled.

The Great Hall at the heart of the Brewery Tap, Chester. Up to eight real ales and at least one cider are served in the 500-year-old building.

company's ales, there were examples from Acorn, Brains, Coach House, Nethergate – and Orchard Pig Marmalade Cider. The building was saved from near collapse in the 1970s. Fully restored, it opened in its present form in 2008 and won the English Heritage/CAMRA Best Conversion to Pub Award the following year. Most food is locally sourced, including smoked produce from the brewery's own smoker. Dog friendly.

By boot and bike: See page 41.

Georgian warehouse suspended above water

Telford's Warehouse, Canal Basin, Tower Wharf, CH1 4EZ. Tel. 01244 390090. www.telfordswarehousechester.com

Seeming to float above the Shropshire Union Canal, it's easy to imagine this cavernous eighteenth-century building humming with activity as crates are winched in and out of barges and labourers manhandle heavy sacks. That activity has long since

Telford's Warehouse, beside Chester's canal basin, is named after engineer Thomas Telford, who designed it in the 1790s. It contained a tavern from its earliest days.

ceased – it was converted to a pub in the 1980s by local architect James Brotherhood and restored following a fire in 2000. A heavy (25cwt) crane remains as a silent memorial to the past in the downstairs bar, with another on the quayside. Dating from the 1790s, it was designed by engineer Thomas Telford for the Ellesmere Canal Company. Construction partially above the water allowed boats to be loaded inside. It contained a tavern from its early days, used by passengers waiting for packet boats to Ellesmere Port. Today, the boat entrance has been glazed, forming a picture window overlooking the historic canal port. The bare brick building, with its massive beams and wooden floors, is open to the roof and has several levels. As well as the cranes, decoration includes a red telephone box, enamel advertising signs and some 3D artworks fashioned from pallets and car components. Six real ales were available, including examples from Elland's, Dark Star, Weetwood, Salopian and Thwaites, plus a large selection of European beers. Meals served; outdoor seating on quayside. Ambient music; regular live music; dog friendly.

By boot and bike: See page 41. *By boat:* Mooring is available opposite the pub.

CHOLMONDELEY, CHESHIRE

Victorian schoolhouse

The Cholmondeley Arms, Wrenbury Road, near Malpas, SY14 8HN. Tel. 01829 720300. www.cholmondeleyarms.co.uk

'Please report to Headmaster' reads the notice painted on the front door. A basket of hockey sticks and tennis racquets awaits the games period. I half expected a bell in the octagonal bell-tower to summon me to assembly. This handsome brick school, and the headmaster's house next door, were built in the 1860s but the last pupils left *circa* 1980. Eight years later it was converted to a pub by the Marquess of Cholmondeley, the first licensed premises on his vast estate for a century or more

Top marks: The Cholmondeley Arms is a school converted to a pub by the Marquess of Cholmondeley. Its interior is well preserved and includes chalked blackboards listing ales served and a monthly 'school quiz.'

(Cholmondeley Castle and gardens are nearby). In 2011 it was restored to a high standard by the present owners, with sandblasted brick walls, repaired cast-iron radiators and beams spanning the high vaulted ceiling. There are wooden floors and a blazing wood fire. Various blackboards indicate beers, menus and events such as a monthly 'school quiz', while vintage local photos include past school portraits. Five well chosen real ales were available on the carved oak bar, including Coach House Gunpowder Mild, Wood's Shropshire Lad and the house Cholmondeley Best, a rebadged bitter from Weetwood of Tarporley. Hundreds of gin bottles decorating the walls indicate the vast choice of this spirit: 320 varieties on my visit, with regular gin tasting classes. Meals are popular and it is advisable to book for dinner. Six bedrooms are available in the Headmaster's House. My breakfast was served by a lady who attended the school as a child and recalled happy times. Garden; dog friendly.

By boot: About 2 miles from the South Cheshire Way along quiet lanes. *By bike:* About 1½ miles from NCN Route 45, Chester-Swindon. Wrenbury Station is 4 miles away.

CLAINES, WORCESTERSHIRE

Old brew-house in a churchyard
The Mug House, Claines Lane, near Worcester, WR3 7RN
Tel: 01905 456649. www.themug.co.uk

Claiming to be one of only two pubs in England on consecrated ground (the other being the Ring o' Bells in Kendal, Cumbria) the Mug House stands in the well-kept churchyard of the parish church, St John the Baptist. Among the graves are those of Sir Edward Elgar's grandparents: the young composer often cycled to Claines on his regular jaunts from Worcester to the Malvern Hills. There are fine views of these uplands from picture windows in the pub's lounge. The building is several hundred years old; originally of wattle and daub construction, part of which can be viewed through a glass panel. The silver head of a medieval bishop's crook and a coin dated 1562 were discovered during restoration work. Thought to have once been the church brew house, beer no doubt contributed to parishioners' morale as well as church funds. According to parish records, riotous festival wakes occurred in the churchyard in medieval times and included bull and bear baiting, dancing and 'drunken roistering.'

The name probably comes from the practice of presenting a mug at one's first Holy Communion. It consists of three rooms – a quarry-tiled and wood-beamed main bar, a carpeted lounge and a rustic snug (converted from a stable) – surrounding a short corridor and central, wood-framed servery incorporating two serving hatches. Reputedly haunted, it has featured on television's *Most Haunted*, with tales of doors banging and other mysterious sounds, including music. The pub cellar, a reputed tunnel linking it with the church, and the Civil War, which was fought bloodily in the area, feature in the stories. It is known for its floral displays in summer and there are two outdoor drinking areas, one facing the churchyard. Four ales were available: Banks's Bitter and Brakspear's Oxford Gold (both usually available) and two guests, the delightful Wychwood Fiddler's Elbow and Ringwood Boon Doggle on my visit. Meals are served at

The Mug House is situated on consecrated ground. It began as the church brew-house and is reputedly haunted.

lunchtime and customers are welcome to bring their own takeaway food in the evening. This is a locals' pub which is also frequented by groups of walkers and cyclists, while the proximity of the church makes it popular after baptisms and funerals (wedding groups set up a marquee). Dog friendly.

By boot: Footpaths and lanes link the pub with the **Monarch's Way and Worcester. This long distance path approximates Charles II's escape route after his defeat at the Battle of Worcester.** *By bike:* On the Worcester to Droitwich section of NCN Route 46.

CLAYGATE, SURREY

Railway station coal office

Platform 3, Claygate Station, The Parade, KT10 0PB. Tel. 01372 462995. www.brightbrew.co.uk

This dolls' house-like structure takes the term micro-pub to an extreme: it is undoubtedly one of the country's smallest pubs. Since there is inside seating for just three customers, thank

Platform 3, the Brightwater Brewery tap, is housed in a former coal office beside Claygate Station.

goodness there is an ample provision of seats and tables on the station forecourt. The handsome adjacent station is served by South West Trains on the Guildford via Cobham and Stoke D'Abernon line from London Waterloo. Platform 3 opened in 2015 in the former coal office, latterly a taxi office, and is run by Alex Coomes and his partner Susan, who also run the local Brightwater Brewery from an outbuilding at their house (Alex is Head Brewer). To make best use of space, a rudimentary bar counter is movable, being set on castors and there is stillage for six casks. Being the brewery tap, Brightwater beers predominate, though only the Daisy Gold (ABV 4%) was available on my winter visit, when opening hours are reduced. Twickenham Small Batch Treacle Stout (4.7%) was also being served. There are also bottled ales and Claygate Cider. A gazebo with heaters is provided in inclement weather, and the outdoor area is decorated with flower tubs in summer. Customers make use of the station toilets. The villagers have taken their

Lilliputian hostelry to heart: it has become a community focal point. Limited opening, usually Thursday through Sunday, subject to weather. No meals; drinks served in plastic glasses; dog friendly.

By boot: There a number of possible walks through this leafy part of Surrey, including Telegraph Hill and the woods and commons to the south (see Ordnance Survey Explorer Map 161).

COLNBROOK, BERKSHIRE

The third oldest inn – and a homicidal medieval landlord

The Ostrich Inn, High Street, near Slough, SL3 0JZ. Tel. 01753 682628. www.theostrichcolnbrook.co.uk

There are countless pubs claiming a ghost but this is the only one we know reputedly once run by a serial killer. Until 2016, there was a model in the bar showing the ingenious contraption the landlord, a Mr Jarman, devised to despatch his guests centuries ago. Claiming to be the country's third oldest inn – the Grade II* building dates from *circa* 1500 but there was a 'hospice' for travellers on the site 400 years before then. Ambassadors once robed themselves here before continuing to meet the king at Windsor Castle nearby. Gnarled wooden beams and remnants of a first floor gallery typical of coaching inns (and now a corridor) are evidence of great age. When Jarman and his wife spotted a suitable target – invariably a single, wealthy traveller on horseback who indicated he was carrying a large sum of cash – they placed him in their best bedroom, above the kitchen. Once he was asleep they released a trap door in the floor, tipping up the base of the bed. The unsuspecting victim fell, head first, into a vat of boiling water. His valuables were stolen, his horse promptly removed and anyone enquiring was told he had departed early. The crimes were discovered when the horse belonging to the last victim was found wandering. At his execution, Jarman boasted he had done away with 60 people.

This model, showing the equipment used by a medieval landlord to murder his guests, was in the bar of the Ostrich Inn until 2016. A tipping bed plunged sleeping victims into a vat of boiling liquid.

An Edwardian postcard view of the Ostrich Inn. Colnbrook was a stop on the stage-coach route between London and Bath.

The dates of the crimes are unknown; they took place between the inn's foundation in 1106 and rebuilding early in the sixteenth century. Some historians believe the account (first told in a book, *Thomas of Reading* by Thomas Deloney, published in the 1590s) is exaggerated. A government return of 1577 places Jarman's inn on the opposite side of the street to the Ostrich, further clouding the tale. A stained glass window depicting a murder taking place now bears silent witness to a macabre legend.

These days the Ostrich is known for its food. I arrived to the appetizing aroma of pan-fried fish. Diners are surrounded by oak beamed partitions and low ceilings. The music room and parlour (used for functions but showing football on a big screen when I visited) are timber-framed delights. The bar, with its ornate wooden counter, has been refurbished recently. The inn was purchased by Kent brewer Shepherd Neame in 2014 and changes in 2016 included new guest bedrooms. Two of the company's cask ales, Spitfire and No. 18 Yard 4-4-2 were available – plus a free booklet describing the inn's history.

By bike: **On NCN Route 61 Maidenhead-Hoddesdon, with a local link to Windsor.**

Edwardian postcard of the Pack o' Cards when it was a hotel called the King's Arms.

COMBE MARTIN, DEVON

House of cards built for an eccentric gambler

The Pack o' Cards, High Street, EX34 0ET.
Tel. 01271 882300. www.packocards.co.uk

This Grade II* listed building was constructed as a residence for local squire, George Ley, in the late seventeenth century. He was a keen gambler and, according to legend, celebrated a large win at the gaming table by commissioning this residence which symbolizes the features of a pack of cards. It had four floors, representing the four suits; thirteen rooms and fireplaces, the number of cards to a suit; and 52 windows and stairs, the number of cards in a deck. It was built on a plot measuring 52ft by 52ft. Some windows were filled in when the Window Tax was introduced but their outline remains. The building's silhouette resembles a house constructed with playing cards and card symbols decorate the eaves on the north side. A sundial on a wall facing the car park is dated 1752 and carries the initials GL for George Ley Junior, who also lived there. It is unclear when it became an inn, but records show that it was in use as such by the early nineteenth century, when it was known as the King's Arms. It did not get its current name until 1933, though locals had called it the Pack o' Cards for a long time. Built of rendered stone, rubble and cob, it has some very old features including a cast-iron balustrade on the top floor, an arched oak door up to 500 years old and ornate ceilings on the first and second floors.

An attractive garden with benches and an adventure playground runs to the river. A flagstone hallway leads to the atmospheric main bar which is carpeted, wood-panelled and has a decorative ceiling above the counter. This has three hand-pumps, serving St Austell Tribute and Charles Wells Bombardier on my visit. There is a modern, glazed conservatory set beneath the rear portico, and two further dining rooms

The Pack o' Cards was built as a residence for a gambling-mad local squire, and incorporates many features of a deck of cards.

provide spacious seating on the other side of the hallway. A separate building houses a skittle alley and exhibition about the inn's history. From this I learned that television personality Michael Parkinson and his wife had their honeymoon there in 1959 and the late magician Paul Daniels took it over in 1987 to film spectacular illusions for the BBC. As you might expect, there are tales of ghosts, too. Apiarists might like to know that the building has the highest number of bee boles (recesses) in the county. Accommodation is also available for humans. Meals served; dog friendly.

By boot: This seaside village is on the South West Coast Path, one of England's most spectacular long distance trails. There are many shorter walks in the area. *By bike:* The 43-mile Culbone Way, crossing Exmoor, also known as regional Route 51 Minehead-Ilfracombe, passes nearby.

CRESSWELL QUAY, PEMBROKESHIRE

Beer served from jugs – pub on remote creek
Cresselly Arms, SA68 0TE. Tel. 01646 651210.

Hidden among folds of wooded hills on a tidal creek in West Wales, this creeper-covered hostelry is worth seeking out. Dating from the mid-eighteenth century, the rambling Grade II listed dwelling became an ale house, the Square and Compass, in the 1780s. The domestic layout is still evident. It was upgraded to a full licence in 1872. Entrance is via a quarry-tiled bar with rustic wooden bar counter and back shelves, simple bench seating and a wood-case clock. You then progress through the former kitchen with its Aga and dartboard, the Hunt Room decorated with horse and hunting prints and trophies, to Alice's Room. This is named after landlady Alice Davies who ran it for twenty years from 1961 (she was serving in her nineties). Alice died, aged 105. Worthington Bitter is served directly from casks racked behind the bar into a jug,

The Cresselly Arms, a former beer house, on its tidal creek in West Wales. The interior still resembles a private house, including seating in the kitchen area complete with Aga.

from which it is transferred to the customer's glass (only one other pub in Wales still serves this way – the Dyffryn Arms, see page 112). Other ales – Purple Moose Snowdonia, Sharp's Doom Bar and Quay Ale, brewed exclusively for the pub by Caffle – were served from hand-pump. There's Welsh cider also. The pub's quay, once a busy inland dock used by coal-carrying vessels, provides an attractive drinking area. Up to 70 vessels sail here, along the Cleddau estuary, during summer river carnivals. Meets of the South Pembrokeshire Hunt also attract hundreds of spectators. During my visit the landlords were preparing for a film crew arriving the following week to film *Their Finest Hour and a Half*, starring Bill Nighy and Gemma Arterton and set in the 1940s. Pembrokeshire CAMRA Pub of the Year 2015. Children and dogs are not allowed; food is served only on special occasions. No ambient music; occasional live bands.

By boot: **Situated on the 60-mile Landsker Borderlands Trail through Pembrokeshire and Carmarthenshire.** *By boat:* **You'll need your own, but it's a wonderful way to arrive, cruising along the Cresswell. The pub has its own moorings.**

DEFFORD, WORCESTERSHIRE

Thatched cottage just serving cider
The Cider House ('Monkey House'), Woodmancote, Worcestershire, WR8 9BW. Tel. 01386 750234.

You can have any drink you like here, as long as it's cider or perry. Dating from the seventeenth century, the half-timbered thatched cottage is a rare survivor of the cider-only houses that once dotted the English countryside. No beer or wine is served. It is one of only four such cider houses in the country, according to CAMRA. There is no official name, nor inn sign and there is no bar counter. Drinks are served, directly from the cask, from a half-door at one end of the building. As you've probably guessed, there is no bar room either, with customers sitting in the front garden, surrounded by daffodils and forget-me-nots on

Customers are expected to sit in the garden of the Cider House, Defford. In bad weather they are permitted to use the bake house on the left. Only cider and perry is served.

my springtime visit and listening to birdsong. In inclement weather they retire to a brick-built bakehouse fitted with a wood-burning stove.

The hostelry has been run by the family of landlady Gill Collins for more than 150 years and is known locally as the Monkey House. This comes from a story that a customer, somewhat worse for wear after imbibing, fell into a patch of brambles. When discovered, he claimed he had been set upon by a pack of monkeys, and the tale passed into folklore. The rustic charm of this simple place is quite magical and harks back to the days when all farm hands were paid partly in cider. No food served; no dogs. Limited opening, do check first.

By boot: About 1 mile west of Defford village. It is possible to plan a walk from Pershore (situated on Shakespeare's Avon Way which follows the eponymous river), using local footpaths and minor roads. *By bike:* Pub is on the A4104 mid-way between two NCN routes, Route 442 at Pershore and Route 45 between Worcester and Tewkesbury.

DREWSTEIGNTON, DEVON

Thatched Dartmoor pub with no bar counter
***The Drewe Arms**, The Square, EX6 6QN.*
Tel. 01647 281409. www.thedrewearmsinn.co.uk

Though named in honour of retail magnate Julius Drewe, who commissioned Sir Edwin Lutyens to design nearby Castle Drogo in 1910, this Dartmoor hostelry has long been known as Aunt Mabel's. Mabel Louise Mudge, who died in 1996 aged 101, was almost certainly England's oldest licensee and was still pouring pints at the age of ninety-nine (*Heritage Pubs of Great Britain*, St Albans, CAMRA, 1998, 69). Originally called the New Inn, it was built to house masons building the adjacent village church in the fifteenth century. Mabel and husband Ernest took over as licensees not long after World War I, when the former began her long reign, becoming a West Country legend in the process

The Drewe Arms was originally built to house masons working on the adjacent fifteenth-century church. The inn sign carries the coat-of-arms of the Drewe family, builders and original owners of nearby Castle Drogo.

(Ernest died in 1951). During my visit, four varieties of bitter (including Dartmoor Brewery's moreish Jail Ale) and eight varieties of scrumpy cider, were being served straight from barrels stacked in the small servery. This is divided from the public bar by a wooden screen. There is still no bar counter, just three hatches (one very small indeed) through which drinks are purchased and passed. Journalist Brian Howes remembers when 'special guests were allowed into Mabel's private parlour for a sing-along on the piano, although most were content to sit in the cosy public bar with its basic bench seating and well-used dartboard.' Electricity and mains water were only installed in the 1940s. Things have hardly changed, though there is now a menu of home cooked food and the original kitchen has been converted to a dining room. If you wish to sample a simple hostelry, evocative of times long past and set in a picture-perfect village square, then you would be hard pressed to find a better example. Outdoor seating at front. Accommodation available in pub and bunkhouse in converted stables. On CAMRA's National Inventory of historic interiors.

By boot: **The village is set on the fringes of Dartmoor National Park, so there are many local walking opportunities. The Two Moors Way long distance path between Ivybridge and Lynmouth passes through. The Teign Gorge–Fingle Bridge section is popular.** *By bike:* **South of NCN Route 279 Okehampton-Exeter.**

DUDLEY, WEST MIDLANDS

Brewery home of Dark Ruby, its recipe lost for thirty years

Beacon Hotel (Sarah Hughes Brewery), 129 Bilston Street, Sedgley, DY3 1JE. Tel. 01902 883380.

For those who thought that unspoilt, traditional pubs were no more, the Beacon shines like a lighthouse. It is a 'one off', deserving of its place on CAMRA's National Inventory of

A customer at the Beacon Hotel is served foaming pints of Sarah Hughes' Dark Ruby and Pale Amber from a curious glazed cubicle. Beers come from an adjacent Victorian tower brewery.

historic interiors and boasting a Victorian tower brewery in its back yard. Sights and sounds such as casks being manhandled over cobbles are accompanied by heavenly brewery aromas. Steam rises mysteriously from an upstairs window. Not much has changed since Sarah Hughes bought the business in 1921 and many of the fittings, such as cast-iron fireplaces, probably date from the hotel's 1850 origin. A glazed island cubicle forms the servery: customers order their drinks through three sliding hatches. Radiating from this are several rooms. There's a front snug with piano, a large rear smoke room with upholstered bench seating and wood panelled walls; and a quarry-tiled hallway. A tap room at the front, with its range, was probably once a kitchen. Modern additions, including a palm filled conservatory, date from a 1987 refurbishment but don't distract from the overall ambience. Conversation is king – there is no ambient music or television. Toilets are outside in the yard. There were two guest beers on my last visit but most customers come for the Sarah Hughes brews: Pale Amber, Surprise or Dark

Ruby (ABV 6%). The latter is a strong Black Country mild, once downed by the area's industrial workers and now sought by discerning drinkers from near and far. Sarah's original recipe was lost for thirty years, until it was discovered in a cigar tin in a bank vault by her grandson John. He adhered closely to it – a closely guarded secret – when the brewery was revived. I found it had the smooth taste of ripe plums with a rich, treacly 'kick' towards the end. In the words of a fellow customer, one of a group that had come from Coventry to try them all: 'It's a perfect beer for last knockings, just before you go home.' I didn't want to go home and I can't wait to get the bus back from Wolverhampton. No meals served but there are cobs, except on Sundays. Closes in the afternoon; garden with play equipment. Brewery tours by arrangement (01902 883381).

By boot: **It is a few minutes' walk to Beacon Hill, one of the highest points in the West Midlands at 778ft, marked with a tower erected in the 1840s.**

Moved 6 miles but the year (1910) hasn't changed

Bottle and Glass, Black Country Living Museum, Tipton Road, DY1 4SQ. Tel. 0121 557 9643. www.bclm.co.uk

Sawdust and spittoons on bare floorboards, a blazing stove, candles and oil lamps for illumination and a glass of dark mild on the table. To say I had gone back in time sounds like a cliché but, in a way, I had. The Bottle and Glass not only exists in a time-warp, in 1979 (the year it closed) the former Ansells house was moved, brick-by-brick, a distance of 6 miles. It migrated from the top of the '16 locks' at Brockmoor on the Stourbridge Canal, to become part of the heritage village in the Black Country Living Museum. The spacious, open-air attraction recreates the area's domestic and industrial past, from buildings even bigger than this, down to the smallest detail. The hostelry has three main rooms: a tap-room described above, a quarry-tiled snug, with a large fireplace and high-backed settles and a more formal back bar complete with piano, cast-iron tables and aspidistras. Changes have been minimal, to comply with

The Bottle and Glass was moved brick-by-brick to its current location from a spot beside the Stourbridge Canal.

environmental health regulations. The pub in its original guise, dating from the 1870s, once had a brewery at the back but this was closed many years previously and there is now a cobbled yard with bench seating. Ales, including mild and bitter, are served through a 'London Pattern' beer engine and are from the local Holden's Brewery; also real cider. As you would expect in a pub set in 1910, there is no Coca-Cola and no electricity. You can, however, catch an Edwardian tram just up the street. Open during museum hours (closes 4pm), museum admission payable. Outside seating.

By boot: **The museum is south-west of Pitchfork Bridge on the Birmingham Canal towpath.** *By bike:* **NCN Routes 5 and 54.** *By boat:* **Electric narrow boats, operated by the Dudley Canal Trust, take visitors from the museum into limestone caverns under Castle Hill (not included in admission charge).**

Snug unchanged in ninety years

Britannia (Sallie's), 109 Kent Street, Upper Gornal, DY3 1UX. Tel. 01902 883253.

Passing the lounge and bar (modern extensions converted from a house and butcher's shop respectively) and entering the back room, I found myself in a panelled snug barely changed since the 1920s. This immaculate space, which resembles the smoking room of an Edwardian house, was originally the tap-room of a family run brewery. In a peculiar arrangement I have not seen elsewhere, four hand-pumps are fixed to the wall beside the door. There is no counter, but an antique wooden servery inlaid with mirrors, complete with shelves for glasses, drawers and a pre-decimal cash-register. Drip-trays and other fittings are of pewter. Ale is only served here on busy evenings, but the room is always accessible. Relaxing after a long walk

from the Crooked House at Himley (q.v.) and sitting on the upholstered bench seating with a pint of Batham's Mild (ABV 3.5%) in hand, I admired the bay window, polished wood fire surround and wood-case clock. What bliss! Had I died and gone to Heaven? On cue, the clock, and others in the pub, began chiming out the hour like celestial bells. There is a secluded garden housing the former brewhouse. The pub, dating from the 1830s, was owned by the Perry family for more than a hundred years, until the death of Sallie in 1992, having been landlady since 1942. It was bought by Daniel Batham's Delph Brewery five years later. On CAMRA's National Inventory of historic interiors. Cobs are served at weekends, pork pies and Scotch eggs at other times. Dog friendly.

By boot: **You are recommended to obtain a free Dudley Real Ale Trail Guide (from local information points or download from www.dudley.gov.uk) and plan your own pub crawl. Local bus services are good.**

The cosy snug at the Britannia, Upper Gornal, showing its antique wooden servery (complete with pre-decimal cash register). This scene has hardly changed since the 1920s and the pub's garden contains an original brew house.

Stove-enamelled ceiling in quirky brewpub

Old Swan (Ma Pardoe's), 89 Halesowen Road, Netherton, DY2 9PY. Tel. (01384) 253075.

'Most tourists lie on the floor to get the best photograph,' said a local who noticed me taking snaps of the stove-enamelled panels covering the bar's expansive ceiling. I didn't fall for the trick and the regulars missed out on a laugh at my expense. I am full of admiration for this unspoilt pub. It takes its nickname from the venerable Doris Pardoe, licensee until 1984. In the centre of the cleverly engineered ceiling is the eponymous Swan. Other antiques to be spotted include a weighing machine, a central stove (its flue running horizontally) and a working steam whistle from the landlord's traction engine. Hand-pumps are devoid of pump-clips in the traditional manner; an ornate Victorian bar-back incorporates a mirror depicting an etched swan and, nearby, an enamel sign declares 'the ales brewed at this establishment are the purest in the borough'. While brewing ceased for a decade or so, it restarted

Swan upper: The Old Swan in Netherton has an eye-catching ceiling, decorated with stove-enamelled metal. Black Country specialities, such as faggots and peas and black pudding, are served, along with home-brewed ale.

in 2001 and it is possible to quaff Old Swan, Dark Swan, Old Swan Entire and Bumble Hole Bitter, knowing they have made but a short journey from the brewery down the hallway. The rear smoke room is a time-capsule, with upholstered bench seating, bell pushes, enamelled glass and sepia portraits of Mrs Pardoe. A former off-sales window, set in a narrow gap, incorporates a bench seat for customers pausing for a quick one before departing with their take-away. A restaurant area was converted from a shop and serves a menu including Black Country specialities such as homemade faggots and peas and black pudding. On CAMRA's National Inventory of historic interiors. Outside yard; upstairs function room; dog friendly.

By boot: A walk of a few hundred yards takes you to a replica of the giant anchor built for the RMS *Titanic* and information panels about this local industry.

DUNGENESS, KENT

Original built with timbers from a wrecked ship
The Pilot Inn, Battery Road, Lydd-on-Sea, TN29 9NJ.
Tel. 01797 320314. http://thepilotdungeness.co.uk

A vast coastal expanse of desert-like shingle, Dungeness is a place like no other. Its features include lighthouses, scattered fishermen's cottages – and a nuclear power station. It is traversed by steam trains on the country's longest miniature railway, the Romney, Hythe & Dymchurch, which pass this pub. The Pilot has been much altered and extended since an original beer house on the site, *circa* 1623, was built or enlarged using the timbers of an ill-fated vessel that met its end on the shingle. An aging exhibit in the bar claims that the Spanish frigate *Alfresis,* carrying gold, wine and spirits, was lured ashore by wreckers and the crew murdered. Its hull was used to form the ceiling of the saloon bar. Today, the main ceiling in the bar is indeed of wood, and hull shaped: it is claimed that some of the original timbers remain. I have enjoyed excellent fish and chips here on two occasions (the Pilot has a well-deserved reputation in this department). Also, it's one of the few hostelries where one can still play the traditional game of Ringing the Bull. This involves accurately swinging a 'nose ring' attached to a string so that it lands on a hook on the wall. It is notoriously difficult and, according to pub games blog *Shove It, Chuck It, Toss It,* is rarely played now, due to the large amount of space required. Three ales were on hand-pump, including Theakston Double Cross IPA and Adnams Broadside, plus Thatcher's Cider. Outdoor seating.

Customers at the Pilot, Dungeness, can play the traditional pub game of Ringing the Bull.

By boot: There are many areas you can walk on Dungeness National Nature Reserve but be prepared for difficulty because of the shingle. A linear walk can be combined with a return ride on the Romney, Hythe & Dymchurch Railway, which also carries bikes. *By bike:* The roads in the area, and surrounding Romney Marsh, are level and generally carry little traffic, making them ideal for circular tours.

EDGEHILL, WARWICKSHIRE

Gothic castle overlooking a battlefield
The Castle Inn, near Banbury, Oxfordshire, OX15 6DJ.
Tel. 01295 670255. www.castleatedgehill.co.uk

This mock-Gothic octagonal tower-house, complete with a 'drawbridge' linking two parts, stands in a commanding position overlooking the site of the first battle of the Civil War (1642). Construction began to mark the battle's centenary on the site where King Charles raised his standard before the clash. Though built as a private retreat for the owner of nearby

A postcard of 1908 shows the Castle Inn at Edgehill with two horse-drawn vehicles outside. The drivers are presumably inside having a pint.

The Castle Inn, Edgehill was built as a private residence but became an inn in 1822. The misty plain below is site of a decisive Civil War battle.

Radway Grange, it has been an inn since 1822. The local Hook Norton Brewery took it over a hundred years later. A sympathetic refurbishment, which included a new conservatory with a bird's-eye view of the countryside (up to 12 counties seen on a clear day) led to a 2015 CAMRA Pub Design Award. Though, from the outside, it's an unlikely-looking public house, those who just wish to drink are welcome: the focal point is a traditional bar. Three Hook Norton ales were on hand-pump. It has a stone floor, a real fire and seats in a cosy watchtower. There is a wood-panelled lounge and dining room (booking advised). Decoration includes several items of replica Civil War armour and swords, plus historical photos. There is a large garden with the same great views. Cyclists and walkers were among the customers. Accommodation.

By boot: The village is on the Centenary and Macmillan Ways, which go along Edge Hill ridge. The inn has a free Civil War Walk leaflet, also on its website (1¾ miles, one hour) taking in the battlefield environs and the Radway Church 1642 exhibition. *By bike:* NCN Route 48 Lincoln to Exeter is planned to go through nearby Radway.

EDINBURGH, LOTHIAN

'On the tiles' with great inventors
Café Royal, West Register Street, EH2 2AA.
Tel. 0131 556 1884. www.caferoyaledinburgh.co.uk

The highlight of this ornate Victorian pub is its series of Faience tiled murals by Royal Doulton, depicting inventors with their discoveries. You can drink in the company of James Watt and his business partner Matthew Boulton, demonstrating their condensing steam engine; George Stephenson with a steam locomotive; Michael Faraday illustrating electro-magnetism; Robert Peel experimenting with calico printing; Benjamin Franklin, 'distinguished in science and politics'; William Caxton who brought printing to England and, in the adjacent bar, Daguerre and Niepce, joint pioneers of photography. They were purchased by an early licensee from the city's International Exhibition of Industry, Science and Art in 1886. The Baroque

Capital pub: Edinburgh's Café Royal is one of Scotland's most opulent hostelries. This view of the Circle Bar shows tiled murals of inventors on the left, with part of the octagonal serving counter on the right.

building, dating from 1862, was designed by Robert Paterson as a showroom for gas and sanitary fittings company Robert Hume, but was probably never used as such. It was taken over by the owner of the North British Hotel (now the Balmoral) as the new site for his Café Royal. The main Circle Bar, in which most of the murals are displayed, also features an octagonal serving counter set with eight brass lamps and, behind it, an ornate gantry. The splendour continues with a marble tiled floor, a decorative gilt-edged ceiling, leather-covered semi-circular seating bays and a marble fireplace. On the other side of a beautiful walnut screen, inlaid with mirrors and etched glass, is the Oyster Bar (an upmarket restaurant) boasting more tiled murals and large stained glass windows depicting British sportsmen. It has a decorative ceiling, a marble topped bar counter, tiled floor and a revolving entrance door.

There are eight hand-pumps in the Circle Bar and the ales served on my visit included Caledonian Edinburgh Castle, Broughton Greenmantle and Exciseman's 80/-, Scottish Borders Flower of Scotland and Kelburn Red Smiddy. I counted 35 malts on the whisky menu and there is a good wine list. The menu specializes in seafood, featuring oysters, mussels, fish stew and Scottish salmon. Ambient music.

By boot and bike: **A few minutes' walk or cycle from Waverley Station. An Edinburgh World Heritage Map, ideal for walkers and cyclists, can be downloaded free of charge at www.ewht.org.uk. Cycle hire is widely available in the city.**

An eclectic collection and strict rules for customers

Canny Man's (Volunteer Arms), 237 Morningside Road, EH10 4QU. Tel. 0131 447 1484. www.cannymans.co.uk

This is like walking into the rambling home of an eccentric uncle. Not that the large brass plaque outside the stone-built hostelry is particularly welcoming: 'No smoking, no credit cards, no mobile phones, no cameras, no backpackers'. Landlord Watson Kerr, who passed away in 2011, went further, imposing

The front bar of Canny Man's in Edinburgh has musical instruments, a battleship, moose's head and Chinese parasol on display.

not only a strict dress code on customers but ejecting anyone who was inebriated, scruffy or expressed radical left-wing views. On my visit I found a complete contrast, the staff being friendly, helpful and tolerant. They will even let you take photos if you ask politely. The two-bar pub has a warren of small rooms set out with vintage furniture and an assortment of paraphernalia that would do justice to a museum. Musical instruments, boats and a bicycle hang from the ceiling; antique bottles and jars line shelves and wall space is filled with wood-case clocks, swords, muskets, corkscrews, vintage prints, ceramics, tools and even electrical switchgear. Nothing was bought: items were donated or pledged in return for drinks. The Churchill Room has memorabilia left by World War II servicemen, while the Smoke Room, with its own bar, has tables set with white tablecloths and fresh flowers. The gents' toilet has a brass 'penny in the slot' device on the door and the front page of the day's newspaper posted above the urinals. Four real ales were served on my visit: Caledonian Deuchars and Castle, Timothy Taylor Landlord and Innis & Gunn Original. There are some 200 malt whiskies behind the bar.

Canny Man's is cared for by the same family that ran it as the Volunteer's Rest in 1871. James Kerr was a drayman for Usher's Brewery; his son John changed the name to the Volunteer Arms but his nickname, the Canny Man, stuck. Son Jimmy took over until the latter's death in 1989, whereupon Watson Kerr took up the reins. On his death, a newspaper obituary described him as 'innkeeper extraordinaire of Edinburgh.' The pub is now run by his widow and sons. Free snacks are served to customers during the day and this extends to a complimentary buffet served at about 5pm (Monday to Thursday). The main food menu is Danish-style smørrebrød, consisting of some 90 dishes, 'all served cold but delicious'. Booking is advisable. There is a patio garden beside the former stables. Ambient music; Havana cigars; dogs at discretion of staff.

By boot: About thirty minutes' walk from Princes Street, passing Bennet's Bar, with its fine interior, in Leven Street on the way. On several bus routes.

In the style of a Greco-Roman temple
***The Dome**, 14 George Street, EH2 2PF.
Tel. 0131 624 8624. www.thedomeedinburgh.com*

The Scottish capital seems to have a greater concentration of palatial pubs than anywhere else in Britain and none is more palatial than this Victorian establishment in the New Town. Entering through an imposing frontage, complete with its Corinthian portico, customers find themselves in a square hall with Ionic columns, twin staircases and a large chandelier. Once through a further doorway they are in the spacious main hall with its arched ceilings and massive central dome. Built in the style of a Greco-Roman temple, it is complete with columned screens at each arm of the cross, and a marble mosaic floor. Beneath the dome is a circular bar counter and gantry, while to the left is a replica of a 1930s Art Deco cocktail bar from an ocean liner (both added in the mid 1990s). Though the rear section is laid out as an upmarket restaurant, the Grill Room, the remainder operates as a bar with several draught ales available (from Caledonian, Sharp's and McEwans on my visit), as well as cocktails and Champagne and wine by the glass or bottle. Nibbles such as peanuts or popcorn are often provided free of charge. The architecture is the work of David Rhind, who built this breathtaking edifice in 1846-7 for the Commercial Bank of Scotland, to serve as its headquarters. Following two banking mergers and the loss of its designation as 'head office', the Royal Bank of Scotland put it up for sale in 1993. It was bought by Caledonian Heritable Ltd., who opened its current stately guise in 1996. There are impressive floral displays, while a large Christmas tree features beneath the dome each December. There is also a Club Room and, upstairs, a Tea Room serving afternoon tea. Ambient music.

By boot and bike: See Edinburgh Café Royal, page 56.

Pleasure dome: The Dome in Edinburgh is built in the style of a Greco-Roman temple and was originally a bank headquarters.

Anchorage of a washed-away pier

Old Chain Pier, 32 Trinity Crescent, Newhaven, EH5 3ED.
Tel: 0131 552 4960   http://oldchainpier.com

This was once a booking office for steamers providing pleasure trips on the Firth of Forth. To reach their boats, passengers would have to negotiate a rickety chain pier behind the building, its walkway just four feet wide. Built in 1821, it was destroyed during a storm that raged for three days in 1898. Inside, I found a foundation stone, complete with iron fixings, that once provided anchorage for the precarious structure. Though the pier itself has gone, there are superb views across the firth from picture windows the length of the bar. The single-storey building consists of three sections: the main bar, a mezzanine and conservatory. It has a cosy feel, enhanced by candle-lit tables, historical photos of the area, glass cases with items for sale and a well stocked bar. Primarily a dining pub, with a menu of locally sourced dishes (reservations are advisable) drinkers are welcome too. Four ales were on hand-pump (two from West Lothian brewery Alechemy, plus Sharp's

The Old Chain Pier, once a paddle-steamer booking office, has fine views of the Firth of Forth.

Doom Bar and Caledonian Deuchars IPA). The building housed a bar from its earliest days, and the licensed premises were enlarged when the boats stopped calling in 1838. Run for many years by the Moss family, in the early 1970s its landlady was Betty Moss, an eccentric who wore bamboo framed glasses and reputedly called time by brandishing a sword or starting pistol, according to her mood. The building has seen several changes: a conservatory was added in 1998; after a fire in 2004 there was some rebuilding, and a further enhancement in 2012. A harbour with its former fish market, now a seafood restaurant but once frequented by the Newhaven 'fish wives' who sold herring from wicker baskets – is a short walk away. Ambient music; live folk music; dog friendly.

By bike: NCN Route 75 to Edinburgh, Glasgow and beyond starts in Leith, a mile east.

This rickety Chain Pier led from what is now the eponymous Edinburgh pub. Its anchor-stone can still be seen in the bar but the structure itself was destroyed in a storm that raged for three days.

EXMINSTER, DEVON

Car-free pub between canal and estuary

Turf Hotel, Turf Lock, EX6 8EE.
Tel. 01392 833128. www.turfpub.net

Known simply as 'the Turf', this is a rare pub indeed as it cannot be reached by car. One can get there by boat, or by boot or bike along the Exeter Canal towpath. I used my folding

The Turf Hotel is marooned between the waters of the Exeter Ship Canal (foreground) and Exe Estuary beyond.

Brompton bike from Exeter and agree with the *Guardian* newspaper, which declared the 7-mile jaunt to be one of Britain's best bike rides. Offering superb views of both the canal and the estuary, widening in anticipation of the sea, the spacious garden is a wonderful place in which to while away a summer's afternoon. The hostelry has several public rooms, with big windows and a central servery that offers several West Country ales (including Otter on my visit) as well as local cider. A wood-burning stove and coal fire provide warmth on cooler days. Period photographs of the locality are dotted around. A local told me that, during World War II, a large number of coffins were stored in the pub's shed in case Exeter suffered a high fatality rate in Nazi bombing raids. Opening times are limited from October-March, so do check before making a journey. Bed and breakfast accommodation.

By boot: There is a footpath from Exminster, or use the Exe Estuary Trail, which is part of the South West Coastal Path. *By bike:* The largely traffic-free Exe Estuary Trail (part of NCN Route 2) takes you round the estuary from Dawlish to Exmouth. Use the ferry to Topsham to complete a loop, if required. A convenient (nearer) start point is Exeter (7 miles) and the Double Locks pub is a pleasant stop around half way. *By boat:* The 'Sea Dream' runs a ferry service from Topsham Quay. There are also cruises from Exmouth to Exeter via the Turf, run by Stuart Line Cruises. See pub website for links and more information. See also Topsham, page 127.

FANCOTT, BEDFORDSHIRE

A ride-on miniature railway

The Fancott (formerly Fancott Arms), Luton Road, near Toddington, LU5 6HT. Tel. 01525 872366. thefancott.co.uk

If you fancy a break from drinking and dining, you can enjoy a train ride around the tree-lined garden of this rural hostelry. It's a phoenix risen from the ashes, since a fire in pub outbuildings destroyed much of the Fancott Miniature Railway's rolling

A miniature railway at the Fancott has its terminus next to the pub and runs for a quarter-mile around the garden. The layout includes an engine shed, signal cabin and level crossing.

stock in March 2015. After lots of hard work, it was reopened a few months later, complete with replacement locomotives and engine shed. A band of volunteers keeps trains on the move, mainly at weekends and school holidays (except Mondays) during the season. Passengers enjoy spotting toys and cuddly animals at the lineside, as they ride the quarter-mile long circuit of 7¼-inch gauge track. There's a station at the end of a reversing triangle, a signal box, footbridge and level crossing. The pub, with a wood-beamed bar and fireplace containing a wood-burner, has expanded into a family dining venue, with contemporary decoration and furniture. There is plenty of room for outdoor dining at front and back, where the railway, lawns and play area are situated. Two real ales were available, St. Austell Tribute and Sharp's Doom Bar. An early version of the railway opened from 1975-86 but the present incarnation dates from 1996, when it was opened by the three-year old son of the pub's owners. Train enthusiasts should also see the Fenn Bell Inn, St Mary Hoo (page 118).

By boot: **The Icknield Way – claimed to be the oldest road in Britain – passes to the north and the Chiltern Way crosses at Chalton, about a mile south-east.** *By bike:* **North of NCN Route 6 Watford-Threlkeld at Houghton Regis.**

FAULKLAND, SOMERSET

Its name recalls a macabre burial – and there's no bar

Tucker's Grave Inn, Wells Road (A366), BA3 5XF.
Tel. 01373 834230.

One of just a few remaining traditional pubs without a bar counter, this is an eighteenth-century stone cottage that has been a beerhouse for more than 200 years. It stands beside a quiet country crossroads and is named after one Edwin Tucker who took his own life in 1747 and is reputedly buried close by. The location was probably chosen because it was once common to bury suicides (who could not be interred on consecrated ground) at crossroads. There are three rooms: a cosy tap room

The public bar at Tucker's Grave Inn doubles as a cellar. Beer and cider casks are kept beside the window and customers sit on settles (behind the camera). The pub featured in a song by the Stranglers.

and a lounge which was formerly a living room. The heart of the pub, however, is a small public bar which doubles as a ground-floor cellar. It has a wood-and-tile fire surround, wooden settles and a single dining table. Casks of beer and cider are stored in a bay window, and the two ales (both from Somerset's Butcombe Brewery) and Thatcher's cider are served straight from them. It was a pleasure to sit with my pint, surrounded by tankards and free-range eggs for sale, chatting to the landlady while a new cask was being expertly tapped with a mallet, just a few feet away. So it once was in countless pubs, but now mainly happens out of sight in a hidden cellar. Many customers were enjoying the richly-coloured local cider and the place was busy soon after opening at 6pm. A fellow customer told me he always visits after volunteering at Glastonbury Festival (the pub features in a haunting song by The Stranglers, who have played here). The view from the rose-filled, stone-walled garden must be one of the finest in the county: a sweeping vista of fields and trees. A skittle alley is housed in a separate building; shove ha'penny is also played. On CAMRA's National Inventory of historic interiors. Outside toilet; no meals; no dogs. There is camping in an adjacent field.

By boot: You can use footpaths to walk from Norton St Philip (q.v.). *By bike:* Situated south of NCN Route 24 Bath–Warminster.

GATESHEAD, TYNE AND WEAR

Coffin-shaped – and a railway roof terrace
The Central, Half Moon Lane, NE8 2AN.
Tel. 0191 478 2543. www.theheadofsteam.co.uk

'You want the coffin pub, pet,' said a local I asked for directions from Gateshead Interchange. This must be the most strangely-shaped pub in the country: a three-storey tall wedge of stone built in 1856, squeezed into an impossibly narrow site between a railway viaduct and two roads near the Tyne and High Level Bridges. Since a £1 million restoration in 2010, the former Victorian hotel has been a pub in the Head of Steam chain;

The Central is a 'wedge of stone squeezed between a railway viaduct and two roads' in Gateshead. There are unusual features inside, too.

highly regarded for its large range of real ales, ciders and whiskies. I counted nine hand-pumps in the main bar alone, with ales from Copper Dragon, Harviestoun, Titanic, Maxim and Camerons and others. The pub is on CAMRA's National Inventory of historic interiors and has several remarkable features. They include a triangular-shaped snug at the pointy end of the 'wedge' and behind the Buffet Bar, which has an ornate 'U'-shaped bar counter and ornate bar-back in polished mahogany. It also boasts a roof terrace where the customer finds himself confronting Newcastle-bound trains high on the adjacent viaduct. As a further nod to railway enthusiasts, the garden contains a model of a British Railways 0-6-0 steam engine and auto-coach. Downstairs, the long, narrow main bar is decorated with historic railway posters, maps and prints of the age of steam by A. E. Gills. Visited on a Friday evening, the pub was full of workers and students from a nearby college, snooker was being played in the upstairs games room and there was a student meeting taking place in the snug. Full of life, in fact; certainly not what you'd expect in a coffin-shaped building. Meals served; dog friendly.

By boot and bike: Situated a few hundred yards from the 14-mile Keelman's Way (NCN Route 14) between Wylam Station and Bill Quay, along the south bank of the Tyne.

GELDESTON, NORFOLK

Isolated and off-grid
The Locks Inn, Locks Lane, NR34 0HS (satnav location)
NR34 0HW (postal). Tel. 01508 518414.
www.geldestonlocks.co.uk

Few pubs occupy a spot as lonely as this. The Locks is set on an islet at the head of the navigable section of the River Waveney, 3 miles upstream of Beccles, Suffolk. I came upon it, sandwiched between the Geldeston and Barsham Marshes, after a wind-blown hike from the town, following the Angles Way. Spring gusts were bending the reeds sideways on the riverbank

The isolated Locks Inn, with the reed-fringed River Waveney in the foreground. Beer is sometimes delivered by boat.

and a heron took flight, like a prehistoric reptile, as I crossed the last two narrow footbridges to reach my goal. For many years, this was a popular haunt of wherrymen, poachers and supporters of illegal prize-fighting. It began as a mill-keeper's cottage, then a lock-keeper's, and got its first licence in the seventeenth century. For thirty-five years, until the early 1970s when she died aged seventy-seven, it was a simple beer-house run by the redoubtable Miss Susan. She suffered hardships such as floods which forced her upstairs, from where she would have to be rescued by boat. She could tell a tale or two – such as that of Black Shuck, a great dog said to haunt the marshes. That tradition is continued today with monthly storytelling by candlelight. The illumination in the main bar is always by candle power: the inn is off-grid and must generate all its own electricity, so it is used sparingly. On cooler days, a wood-burner blazes in a cavernous fireplace.

Though it has been extended over the years, the heart of the place remains a quarry-tiled, wood-beamed bar, furnished with time-worn settles and historical local photos. An indoor room is available for bands when the weather is not suitable for performance in the garden. Live music, including folk, is a regular feature. The barman told me about a third of customers arrive on foot and another third use the little 12-person, electric ferry boat from Beccles. The remainder negotiate a long, unmade track from the village by car or bike. Whichever way you come, it's well worth the effort. Beer casks are sometimes delivered by boat. Three ales were available on my visit, the regular Oak from Norfolk's Grain Brewery, Cascadian Blonde from Tempest and Free State from Brighton Bier. Real cider; meals served; dog friendly; ambient music. Reduced opening in winter.

By boot: Pub is a quarter-mile north of the Angles Way, a 93-mile trail following the Norfolk-Suffolk border between Great Yarmouth and Thetford. It is 3½ miles from Beccles by this path, or you can take the longer Waveney path (5 miles). A map of local walks is displayed outside the pub. *By bike:* Situated south of the Halesworth to Norwich section of NCN Route 1 and regional route 30. *By boat:* Big Dog Ferry operates from May to September from Beccles Lido (www.bigdogferry.co.uk, 01502 712160, booking advised). There's plenty of wildlife to see en route. Free overnight mooring adjacent to pub; canoe hire available locally.

GLASGOW, STRATHCLYDE

Not just haunted – home to a paranormal society
The Scotia, 112 Stockwell Street, G1 4LW.
Tel. 0141 552 8681. http://scotiabar.net

Situated a few blocks north of the River Clyde, this claims to be the city's oldest pub, originating as a sailors' tavern in 1792. Don't be fooled by the box-like frontage: the interior is very different, little changed since 1929. Reminiscent of an old

The Scotia's frontage is functional but the interior, meeting place for Glasgow's Other Side, is delightful.

GUILDFORD, SURREY

The first purpose-built car factory
The Rodboro' Buildings, 1–10 Bridge Street, GU1 4RY.
Tel. 01483 306366. www.jdwetherspoon.co.uk

sailing ship below decks, there are nooks and crannies, and wood panelled walls beneath varnished beams. There are lots of historic photos. Though I called at six on a damp, dark afternoon, the place was busy and lively. By all accounts, it always is. The Scotia is known for its live music, local lads Billy Connolly and the late Gerry Rafferty being among past performers. It is a retreat for folk musicians and writers and, for a long time, an annual Poet Laureate competition was held, though sadly this has been discontinued. Not only is the bar reputedly haunted but a paranormal investigation society, Glasgow's Other Side, has met regularly for many years (currently on the first Tuesday of the month). It has probably been subject of more ghost hunts by television programmes and psychic groups than any other Scottish bar. So many, in fact, that they have called a hiatus: 'I've been told that people feel these investigations have disturbed the spirits,' said manager Mary Rafferty. Nevertheless, keep an eye out for a young boy running in and out of a door and the Victorian 'green lady', a former barmaid who wears a velvet dress and plumed hat. No real ale; lunches on certain days.

By boot: The 40-mile Clyde Walkway goes through the city's heart – this was once the second city of the British Empire – to the World Heritage Site of New Lanark.

I could imagine the whirr of drive belts, the clatter of hammers and the smell of paint and varnish as I sat in this cavernous monument to the motor-car. It was originally the specially built factory of Dennis Brothers Ltd., bicycle and motor vehicle manufacturers, operating from 1901-11. The company became best known for its buses, fire engines, commercial vehicles and military tanks. Later, the building became a footwear manufactory (1919-27), followed by many other uses, before being transformed into a 'Lloyds No.1' bar by J.D. Wetherspoon, in 1998. The gracefully curved, listed building had been threatened with demolition. One innovative feature of the Onslow Street Works, as it was known, was a lift allowing

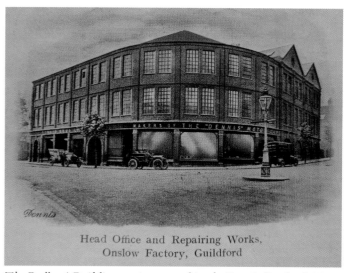

Head Office and Repairing Works,
Onslow Factory, Guildford

The Rodboro' Buildings as it appeared in the Dennis Brothers' 1902 catalogue. Then known as the Onslow Street Works, it served as a combined vehicle factory and showroom.

The Rodboro' Buildings in Guildford has been a cavernous Wetherspoon's pub since 1998. It has been cleverly converted, retaining the atmosphere of its industrial past.

newly assembled vehicles to be moved to the ground floor showroom. Today, customers move between two floors, with bars on each, and there's a lower area which converts to a weekend dance floor. As well as exposed original brickwork and windows, the interior cleverly uses metal girders, lamps and factory lettering to emphasize the building's original use. On the ground floor, partitioned snugs resemble supervisors' offices, with adjacent portraits of John and Sir Raymond Dennis paying tribute to the company's founding siblings. Illuminated technical drawings provide an eye-catching frontage to the bar counters, while illustrated panels inform customers about the history. A selection of nine real ales included Upham Hunter, Hammerpot This England and Dark Star Partridge on my visit. Meals are available all day. Outdoor area, games machines (silent). Music is a feature at certain times. Recognized by the Transport Trust as a Transport Heritage Site.

By boot and bike: The River Wey towpath leads from the centre of town, past Dapdune Wharf (boat trips) and, near Shalford, is the Wey and Arun Canal where you can take the Wey South Path or climb Chinthurst Hill. The 37-mile Downs Link starts outside town, this largely traffic-free route using disused railway routes to link the North and South Downs with the coast at Shoreham-by-Sea.

HALLATROW, SOMERSET

A full-size railway carriage – and some eclectic memorabilia

The Old Station Inn, Wells Road, BS39 6EN.
Tel: 01761 452228. www.theoldstationandcarriage.co.uk

An ex-British Railways Mark I passenger carriage, furnished with armchairs and linen-covered tables, is the focal point of this pub's extended back garden. Installed in the late 1990s, the coach was inspired by the Royal Scotsman luxury train and can be entered directly from the pub. It is just one seating area of this former railway hotel, which served an adjacent Bristol & North Somerset Railway station. This was closed in 1959 and subsequently demolished. Off a central 'island' bar counter are a number of rooms filled with the licensees' growing collection of memorabilia. There is a hat room filled with assorted millinery; a music room where the display majors on musical

A British Railways' passenger coach is the main feature of the Old Station Inn's garden, where it serves as a dining room with a difference.

instruments and, in the main room, lamps and enamel signs feature. The front of a Citroën 2CV car bursts out of one of the walls, headlights blazing. There are old radios, sewing machines and cameras and newspaper cuttings of historical events. Five hand-pumps served, on my visit, several beers from Brains brewery (including Reverend James) and Butcombe Bitter; also real cider. The venue is popular with diners and booking is advised, especially for the carriage. The menu – I enjoyed baked breast of chicken filled with smoked cheese and wrapped in Parma ham – includes homemade desserts. There is a wooded garden with crazy golf and a decking area. Ambient music; dog friendly; accommodation in a converted railway building.

By boot: **Hallatrow is on the Limestone Link, a 36-mile path linking the Cotswold Way with the West Mendip Way.**

The front-end of a Citroën car is one of many unusual objects that decorate the Old Station Inn.

HARROGATE, WEST YORKSHIRE

Naked flames and stuffed animals
Hales Bar, 1-3 Crescent Road, HG1 2RS. Tel. 01423 725570. http://halesbar.co.uk

With two gas jets (cigar lighters) on the bar sending their flames into the air and cases displaying a variety of birds and other animals, this could be the home of an eccentric Victorian taxidermist. Gas lights, polished wood panels, historical photos and bench seating complete the scene. One of the spa town's oldest pubs, this former coaching inn is a four-storey corner building of local stone, rebuilt in the 1820s. It is named after a nineteenth-century landlord, William Hales and was used in the filming of *Chariots of Fire* (1980). Six hand-pumps were dispensing a variety of mainly Yorkshire ales, including Hales Ale (the house bitter by Daleside) and others from Timothy Taylor, Daleside and Black Sheep; also real cider. The antique

Hales Bar, Harrogate: naked flames blaze on the counter and cases of stuffed animals adorn the walls.

bar-back features six wooden spirit vats. I have described the high-ceilinged saloon which is the most atmospheric bar, best enjoyed from one of the alcoves with their high-backed red upholstered benches. There is also a Vaults Bar. Weekly events include a 'gas-lit acoustic afternoon'. Dogs allowed, except when meals are being served.

By boot: The Harrogate Ringway is a 20-mile walk circling the town, passing various points of interest. The Nidderdale Greenway is a 4-mile long traffic-free path to Ripley on a former rail line, crossing the Nidd Gorge Viaduct. *By bike:* The Greenway is also suitable for cyclists (NCN Route 67, which also goes south to Wetherby). NCN 636 connects Harrogate with Knaresborough.

HAVANT, HAMPSHIRE

Reminders of the 'last dancing bear'
The Old House at Home, 2 South Street, PO9 1DA. Tel. 02392 483464. www.oldhouseathomehavant.co.uk

The Old House at Home is Havant's oldest surviving dwelling. Inside, customers can inspect a wooden post to which the 'last dancing bear' was tethered.

This half-timbered hostelry is Havant's oldest dwelling, dating from the early seventeenth century. Two of the many beams above the lounge bar are reputedly from a ship of the Spanish Armada. The main claim to fame is that it was reputedly the last pub in the country to have a dancing bear. The weather-beaten post to which it was allegedly tethered can be seen in the bar, incongruously positioned between a games machine and a flat-screen television, though it was originally outside. A photograph exhibited shows the bear and a handler holding a fiddle. According to one story, the animal was already employed there when brewer George Gale & Company took over the establishment in 1903; it belonged to two French brothers. According to another, it belonged to a German oompah band which was lodging there. Both stories agree on the sorry ending of the episode, however. The bear's owners had to return to their home country on the outbreak of the Great War. They could not find anyone to look after the animal so it was shot in a field at the rear and buried nearby. Today, the open-plan establishment includes a cosy dining area and a large brick fireplace which contained a baker's oven. The pub is now run by Fuller's, which took over Gale's some years ago. Four of the company's ales were available: London Pride, ESB, Wild River and Gale's Seafarers. Meals are served and there is a patio garden; dog friendly.

By boot: There is a Havant Heritage Trail (copies from the town museum), marked by 34 plaques and whose highlights include a former glove factory, a Dissenters' Chapel and a natural spring. I noticed one resident had affixed a home-made plaque to his cottage: 'Sylvia Plath never bought a loaf of bread here.' *By bike:* The former railway to Hayling Island has become a 4-mile, traffic-free trail (part of NCN Route 2). Much of the ride is along the shore. Eastwards, NCN 2 continues towards Chichester; westwards, NCN 22 goes to Gosport.

HERNE, KENT

A butcher's shop – and the original micropub

The Butcher's Arms, 29A Herne Street, CT6 7HL.
Tel. 01227 371000. www.micropub.co.uk

Joints of meat (fake) and chickens (plastic) hang from metal hooks; chopping tables are ready for the bacon slicer. White-tiled walls evoke days when every High Street included a family butcher. Except this is no longer a butcher's shop. It became Britain's first micropub in 2005 when local entrepreneur Martyn Hillier had the idea of turning his off-licence into a small pub offering cask ale, real cider and hearty conversation. Like all such pubs, there are no frills and consequently no unnecessary overheads. Seating is for just 15 customers and standing room for about 20, in a space measuring 3x4 metres. Martyn started a trend – micropubs have since been popping up all over the country and he is well-known as a campaigner for them. I visited with my daughter, then a student in nearby

Meating place: original chopping tables are still in use at the Butcher's Arms, Herne. 'Poultry' hanging from the ceiling is imitation.

Canterbury, bringing our own lunch from a convenience store and enjoying cask ale (choice of four), scrumpy cider, and indulging in banter with the other customers. There was no meat on offer – but we did have some smoky bacon crisps. Winner of several CAMRA awards; dog friendly.

By boot: **Catch a train to Sturry via Canterbury West. If you don't wish to walk the remainder, bus 6 continues to Herne Church, situated opposite the pub. (See also Herne Bay entry.)**

HERNE BAY, KENT

Beach hut on a seaside pier

Beer on the Pier, Hut 31, Herne Bay Pier, CT6 5JN.
Tel. 07443 046813.

What could be more delightful than sitting in a beach hut, drinking real ale and contemplating the sea as a fairground organ plays? A micropub with a difference, it opened in summer 2015 on a pier dating from 1899 and full of family amusements. How many other pubs can offer merry-go-round 'gallopers' and a helter-skelter as amusements for their customers, I wonder? This is run by local brewer Goody Ales, which is developing something of a shed theme as its brewery tap is in a large one known as 'the cathedral'. The hut measures 3x4 metres and incorporates, at the time I visited, two bar stools, bench seating for half-a-dozen, a bookshelf library and a box of games. The maximum number of customers inside was 16 at Christmas 2015 – described as 'very cosy' by manager Jo. Two Goody beers, Good Friday (ABV 4.5%) and Good Heavens (4.1%) were being served straight from the cask and there was local cider from Broomfield. Some bottled beers, including the brewery's own, are available. Outside seating on the pier is popular on a sunny day but tables are devoid of umbrellas (they would take off in the first gust of wind). Opening hours vary according to season and weather conditions (weekends only in winter) – check the pub's Facebook page. A memorial board at

Beer on the Pier is a beach hut seating six customers. Adjacent amusements include a merry-go-round and helter-skelter.

Lean-to: The Crooked House at Himley tilts at an angle of 15 degrees. The author felt queasy before he even had a drop of ale.

the pier entrance commemorates pioneer aviatrix Amy Johnson, who crashed in 1941. Once one of the country's longest, the pier is now much shortened: its stub end is marooned at sea. The resort has two other micropubs at the time of writing, the Bouncing Barrel and Firkin Frog. No meals; dog friendly.

By boot: **The 160-mile Saxon Shore Way from Gravesend to Hastings negotiates the resort, offering some of England's finest coastal walking. There is a Herne Bay Cultural Trail around town.** *By bike:* **The Oyster Bay Trail (regional route 15) passes through towards Reculver, joining the Viking Coastal Trail (q.v.) around Thanet.**

HIMLEY, STAFFORDSHIRE

Leaning pub

The Crooked House, Coppice Mill, near Dudley (off B4176), DY3 4DA. Tel. 01384 238583.

The building's 15-degree tilt that has turned this place into a local attraction is no architect's whimsy but is due to the pub subsiding into an abandoned coal-mine long ago. Thankfully, it has been carefully secured, with buttresses supporting the wilting end and iron bolts and girders keeping the walls intact. Inside, sloping floors and leaning window frames made me feel a little queasy momentarily, but the feeling passed when distracted by novelties such as an empty beer glass moving of its own accord and a demonstration of a marble rolling uphill (effects caused by the building's tilt). I found the location as remarkable as the structure: the setting is reminiscent of a scene from *War of the Worlds*. The approach is along a narrow, winding lane past a foaming stream, spidery trees and under a disused railway, with former mining land and a quarry adjacent. At the end is the solitary pub. A kingfisher flashed by, reassuring me that nature survives, against the odds. The old part of the hostelry, consisting of two quarry tiled, wood-panelled rooms either side of the front door, has been tastefully renovated. There is a wood-fired range in the lounge and lots of information about the place around the walls. At the rear is a large and comfortable modern extension housing a restaurant and conservatory. Two Banks's ales were available (Mild and Bitter) plus the house ale, Crooked House Tilted Tipple (ABV 3.6%) brewed by Marston's. Originally an eighteenth-century farmhouse, it became a pub, Siden House, later renamed the Glynne Arms. After subsiding into a collapsed shaft of the mine workings, the building was condemned in 1940 but purchased by Wolverhampton & Dudley Breweries which saved it from demolition. Restaurant (booking advised); dog friendly (bar only); outside seating; play area.

By boot: The South Staffordshire Railway Walk runs about a quarter-mile south of the pub en route to Pensnett Pools but access directly from it to the pub was not possible at time of writing.

HONEY STREET, WILTSHIRE

HQ for crop circle fans – serving 'Alien' beer

The Barge Inn, near Pewsey, SN9 5PS.
Tel. 01672 851705. www.the-barge-inn.com

Ales of the unexpected: Locally brewed Alien Abduction Green Beer is sold at the Barge Inn. It is popular with 'croppies'.

Its location alone makes this pub worth seeking out. Behind a wood yard beside the Kennet & Avon Canal, overlooking the rolling Wiltshire Downs in the Vale of Pewsey, where a white horse carved out of the hillside forms a backdrop. This is the heart of crop circle country, and the Barge Inn's claim to fame is that it is the spiritual home of the 'Croppies'. Once a year, aficionados from around the world meet here to discuss sightings of these strange but beautiful phenomena – large, artistic pictograms that appear without warning in fields and farmlands. The solid Georgian building of brick and Bath stone, which once also included a brewery, stable and slaughterhouse, is dated 1810 (contemporary with the canal's construction). It was largely rebuilt following a fire in 1858 and, for a long time, was part of the Ushers of Trowbridge estate. It has floors of wood and a mix of rustic furniture, nostalgic items such as sewing machines and musical instruments on display and unusual light fittings. The snooker room will be of interest to most visitors as this is crop circle central. Its ceiling is decorated with a mural of mysterious Wiltshire places – including Stonehenge, Avebury and other stone circles as well as tumuli and the mythical Green Man. It is said the county is home to the greatest concentration of prehistoric monuments in Europe. Around the walls are photographs of crop circles, which are pin-pointed and colour-coded on Ordnance Survey maps. It could almost be a military control room. Outside, on the adjacent campsite, an observatory was taking shape and will one day, I was told, house a telescope beaming pictures from space into the pub. The bar counter has six hand-pumps offering a variety of local beers, several from Honeystreet Ales: Alien Abduction, which is green; Croppie and 1810, while scrumpy lovers can sample Area 51 cider. Food served; ambient music; weekly live music; camping adjacent. A former barn is used for art exhibitions.

By boot and bike: The Kennet & Avon Canal towpath provides pleasant walking and cycling towards Pewsey or Devizes (NCN Route 4 follows this and quiet roads). NCN 45 Chester-Salisbury passes just to the east. *By boat:* The Kennet & Avon Canal links the Avon at Bath with the Thames at Reading; twenty-four-hour moorings outside. The annual Devizes to Westminster Canoe Race passes the pub.

HUISH EPISCOPI, SOMERSET

Thatched pub with no bar counter – in the family for generations
Rose and Crown (Eli's Inn), Wincanton Road, near Langport, TA10 9QT. Tel. 01458 250494

I first visited this pub about fifteen years ago while cycling the Somerset Levels. It was like walking into a friendly family home where the kitchen had been laid out for a drinks party. On returning recently to research this book, I'm pleased to say that it hasn't changed. It is still in the same family ownership, and stepping through the front door onto the stone-flagged floor, to find the various rooms laid out around the central servery, was like coming home. There is no bar counter and customers are welcome to enter this inner sanctum, whose walls are lined with hand-pumps and optics and shelves are stacked with drinks and glasses. Ales included the regular Teignworthy Reel Ale plus Milk Street 'RA' and Cottage Brewing's Starlight. The local Somerset cider and cider brandy are popular. The present stone and thatch building dates from the late eighteenth century, has Gothic windows and is fringed with rose bushes. The various

'Like a family home where the kitchen is laid out for a drinks party': the Rose and Crown dates from the eighteenth century.

parlour rooms are simply furnished with wooden tables and chairs, a piano, dartboard, wood-case clock and old prints and photographs. They include portraits of two soldiers in World War I uniforms: great uncles of the present licensees, killed in action on the Western Front, aged nineteen and twenty-three. The low-lying area suffers regular floods. The barman explained that, though the pub itself has not been flooded for seven years, more recent floods meant that some customers were unable to get near their local without a boat.

The name 'Eli's' relates to Samuel Eli Scott, grandfather of the present owners who, with his wife Maude Lillian Slade, ran the hostelry for many years and died in 1978. There is a garden filled with honeysuckle and roses. Food is served lunchtime and evening. Outdoor toilets; dog friendly.

By bike: **Situated on the Somerset Levels which is mainly flat and, with lightly used minor roads, is popular with cyclists of all ages and abilities. A Somerset Levels cycling map is published by Sustrans.**

ILFRACOMBE, DEVON

Rooftop garden creates a cliff-top illusion
The Admiral Collingwood, Wilder Road, EX34 9AP. Tel. 01271 862373. www.jdwetherspoon.co.uk

The architects of this modern pub, on the seafront of the popular North Devon resort, have borrowed a trick from the landscape gardeners of the eighteenth century. They used a sunken wall called a ha-ha, forming a hidden barrier between a formal garden and a natural landscape, making the scene look seamless. At the Admiral Collingwood, the same thing has been done, using a glass balustrade to surround the first floor roof terrace. It has the effect of making the rooftop look as though it's part of the coastal cliffs. The illusion is enhanced by a carpet of artificial grass. Seating on this terrace includes weatherproof armchairs. Opened in 2014 on the site of a hotel and part of the J.D. Wetherspoon chain, the pub has an unusual design that makes use of bold curves and includes a glass atrium, said to have been inspired by the movement of the sea. Maritime themed artwork adds to the nautical atmosphere. The bright and spacious interior uses a variety of materials including wood, tile and stone, for a contemporary look. It is filled with light from the glazed frontage and the glass atrium, which has a circular seating area beneath. The curved main bar counter has 12 hand-pumps serving a changing selection of guest ales, as well as regulars, such as Greene King Abbot and Sharp's Doom Bar. A smaller upstairs bar serves *al fresco* customers using the rooftop area. I found the service extraordinarily efficient: the dessert arrived at my table before I had returned from ordering it at the bar. Winner of CAMRA's New Build award 2015 for the high standard of its architecture.

By bike and boot: Ilfracombe is situated on the Tarka Trail, one of the country's longest continuous traffic-free walking and cycling paths, part of the Devon Coast to Coast Cycle Route (NCN 27 and 3). For walkers, the South West Coast Path (see also Combe Martin, page 46) offers spectacular scenery. *By boat:* The pub is a short walk from the quay, where boat trips, sea safaris and sailings to Lundy Island depart.

The roof garden of the Admiral Collingwood in Ilfracombe looks like it's part of the coastal cliffs. The cliffs are actually in the distance, the other side of a main road.

KENFIG, MID GLAMORGAN

Remnant of a 'lost town' – the town hall is upstairs

The Prince of Wales, near Bridgend, CF33 4PR.
Tel. 01656 740356. www.princekenfig.co.uk

This isolated stone building is a surviving remnant of a coastal town that has been otherwise lost to storms and shifting sands, like a Welsh version of Atlantis. It was built on pillars in the seventeenth century as the town hall, and the large upstairs Guild Hall Longroom is still used as such by Kenfig Corporation Trust. Guided tours are by the landlord on request. It contains wall panelling from the period as well as a copy of the mayor's mace, local coats-of-arms and wooden benches from the time when it served as a courtroom. It has also been a mortuary when shipwrecks occurred. The pub consists of three rooms, including a restaurant serving local produce, on the ground floor and decorated with historical photos, maritime charts and other local memorabilia. Real ales from Tomos Watkin, Wye Valley and Breconshire Brewery were available on my visit, also Welsh cider.

The Prince of Wales at Kenfig occupies a seventeenth-century building that has the town hall upstairs.

After centuries of storms and raids by Vikings and other invaders, a storm in the early 1600s destroyed what was left of Kenfig. The tops of some of the buildings buried by the shifting sands, including a castle, can sometimes be seen around Kenfig Pool, a freshwater lake, and the nature reserve opposite. Sand dunes and the Bristol Channel stretch out beyond. A plaque in the car park gives some historical information and there is a propeller blade on a plinth, salvaged from a local shipwreck. The distant chimneys and industry of Port Talbot can be seen from the road that approaches the pub. Check opening hours before visiting; meals most days; dog friendly.

By boot: **A 7-mile walk around Kenfig's dune system, including lots of historical and natural interest, can be viewed on www.glamorganwalks.com. The pub is served by bus from Bridgend.** *By bike:* **About 1 mile from the Celtic Trail (NCN Route 4).**

KING'S NYMPTON, DEVON

Thatched pub with 900 bookmarks

The Grove Inn, EX37 9ST. Tel. 01769 580406.
www.thegroveinn.co.uk

To those who grew up with computers, a bookmark is something digital and connected with your internet surfing habits. For those of us brought up on books, it is a tangible object, usually made from paper or leather, that comes in various sizes and is often infused with sentimental value. So it is at the Grove Inn, where the landlord Robert's vast collection of bookmarks makes a powerful visual statement as soon as you enter the thatched seventeenth century pub. Hundreds of them (more than 900 in fact) are lined up in neat rows along the ceiling's rough oak beams. They come in all colours, shapes, sizes and from places near and far, and bearing all manner of imprints. There's even a joke 'Stone Age' bookmark, specially crafted by a sandal maker in a North African souk; and a genuine framed Elizabeth II Coronation bookmark, kept behind

Some of the hundreds of bookmarks decorating the bar of the Grove Inn, King's Nympton.

the bar for reasons of security. Most have been donated by customers who have been inspired by this peculiar gallery, so the collection is growing and may end up taking over the place. The flagstoned floor, rough stone walls and log fire are further attractions, as is the menu making use of local, seasonal produce and the landlord's penchant for locally brewed real ales. Golden Hill Exmoor Ale (ABV 3.8%) is a regular, while guest beers on my visit included Hunter's Devon Dreamer, Otter Summer Light and Sharp's Own, plus there was a choice of at least three local ciders and about 60 malt whiskies. If looking at bookmarks becomes tiring, there's always someone to chat with (this is a community local), the day's enticing menu to pore over and a portrait of the village Home Guard troop (their names carefully appended) from World War II. Darts and other traditional games; dog friendly.

By boot: The pub and village, set in pleasant countryside, are about 2 miles from King's Nympton Station on the 'Tarka Line' railway between Exeter and Barnstaple. The line offers many walking options, allowing you to start and finish at different stations.

LACOCK, WILTSHIRE

Dog-powered roasting spit
The George Inn, 4 West St, SN15 2LH.
Tel. 01249 730263. www.georgeinnlacock.co.uk

Situated in an historic village maintained by the National Trust, this mellow stone and brick hostelry is justly popular with sightseers. There has been an inn here since the fourteenth century and the wood floors, exposed oak beams and fireplaces evoke a bygone age. A well and set of stocks at the rear are also redolent of time when life was tough. The most unusual feature is a roasting spit mounted in front of one of the fireplaces, linked to a large wooden treadmill, halfway up the left-hand wall. A small turnspit dog was trained to run inside this wheel which, in turn, rotated the spit. This special breed of dog had a long body and short, often bandy legs. Though once common in large houses and inns, this is thought to be the only complete example surviving in a pub. The use of turnspit dogs, also known as kitchen- or under-dogs, was first mentioned in the 1570s but was in decline by the late eighteenth century. They would be worked in pairs and one would be inclined to leap out after a given period, to be replaced by his compatriot. They would also be taken to church and used as foot-warmers. A preserved example of the breed can be examined next to the wheel, along with some descriptive text. Also of interest is a gallery of film and television productions and celebrities that have used the inn – Lacock is probably the most filmed village in the country – from the *Cranford*

The original dog treadmill, connected to a roasting spit, in the George Inn, Lacock. A special breed of kitchen-, or under-dog, was trained to turn it.

Chronicles (Judi Dench) to *Harry Potter* (Daniel Radcliffe), from John Craven to Holly Willoughby. The village is little changed since pioneer photographer, and local resident, Henry Fox Talbot recorded it in 1840.

Real ales from Wadworth's are available, plus guests (Hog's Back HBB and Island Brewery Yachtsman's Ale on my visit); also local cider. The menu is a major attraction – most customers appeared to be dining when I called. Extended garden; ambient music; dog friendly.

By boot and bike: Lacock is on the North Wiltshire Rivers cycling and walking route, which is largely off-road from Melksham to Avebury, following NCN Route 4.

LEEDS, WEST YORKSHIRE

Sea-going barge on dry land

The Dry Dock, Woodhouse Lane, Leeds, LS2 3AX.
Tel. 0113 391 2658.   www.thedrydockleeds.co.uk

One doesn't expect to come across a sea-going gravel barge on dry land in a city centre, next to a multi-storey car park. Not only can visitors to Leeds see such a vessel but they can go on board and eat and drink without risk of seasickness. The vessel has been land-locked here since 1993 but retains original features such as portholes, riveted steelwork and the ship's wheel on the bridge. It is held at anchor on a grassy 'sea' next to a wooden 'dock', into which the pub extends. The top deck is claimed to be the city's largest open roof space for drinkers. I found the bare-boards simplicity and food and drink promotions had attracted a student crowd – the university campus is across the road – but I didn't feel out of place. Two ales, Wychwood Hobgoblin and a refreshing Leeds Brewery Pale, were on hand-pump, plus there was real cider.

By boot: The Waterfront Walk follows the River Aire and Leeds & Liverpool Canal from the city centre, taking in lots of restored industrial heritage. For a map see

Bow of the sea-going gravel barge that houses the Dry Dock pub in Leeds. Its entrance is through the 'jetty' on the right.

www.leeds.gov.uk. *By bike:* Leeds is on NCN Route 66, Manchester-Spurn Head. The route is traffic-free between the city and Shipley, using the Leeds & Liverpool Canal towpath. *By boat:* There are well equipped moorings at Leeds Dock (previously Clarence Dock), home of the Royal Armouries and ten minutes' walk from the city centre.

Art gallery with hairdressers attached

Outlaws Yacht Club, 38 New York Street, LS2 7DY.
Tel. 0113 324 6998. http://outlawsyachtclub.com

Despite the name, this is not a yacht club. It is not really a pub either. In the words of its website, it is a 'coffee shop and exhibition space/creative hub.' One that sells alcohol and does hairdressing, I must add. Situated in a modern, glass fronted building close to the city bus station, its open-plan design features artworks on the walls and different kinds of seating. The tables were set with fresh flowers. An ageing silver cash register has pride of place and there are vintage electrical items. The bar was stocked with a variety of craft beers (though not real ale) from around the world. It sells Fairtrade coffee and the staff mix cocktails, too. Artworks and prints are often for sale and exhibitions change regularly. There are board games to play, children's books and Lego available, for those able to put down

The hairdressing section of Outlaws Yacht Club. The bar is a few paces away and customers often enjoy drinks while having their hair done.

The main entrance to Whitelock's Ale House contains one of a fine collection of old mirrors. Ornate panelling, along with fine copper and brass work, is also evident inside.

their mobile phones. In the corner of the room is the entrance to Rebel Pin Up, otherwise known as 'creative hairdressing'. Tall, gilt framed mirrors and a glittering chandelier provide contrast with the rest of the establishment. Customers are welcome to take their drinks into the hairdressers. Late at night the venue takes on yet another persona as a DJ bar and space for live entertainment. Meals served; ambient music; dog friendly.

By boot, bike and boat: See page 74.

Victorian hall of mirrors and tiles

Whitelock's Ale House, Turks Head Yard (off Briggate), LS1 6HB. Tel. 0113 2453950 / 0113 2423368.
www.whitelocksleeds.com

Though secreted in an alleyway off a main thoroughfare, thousands of visitors manage to find their way here. Whitelock's is a Leeds' institution: a hall of antique mirrors, a feast of ornate tiling and banquet of brass fittings. I arrived at 11am on a winter's morning, hoping to have the place to myself but it soon filled up with customers, many eager for fish-and-chips and other specialities of the house. I warmed myself beside the coal fire, admiring portraits of Queen Victoria and some of her eminent subjects. First licensed in 1715 and originally called the Turk's Head, the bar was restored in the late 1800s for the entrepreneurial Whitelock family, who owned it until 1944. The long, narrow layout features a similarly long bar counter, faced with ceramics and topped with marble and copper. Oak beams, polished woodwork, stained glass windows and candy-twist brass stanchions complete the exquisite scene. Being a genuinely free house, there was a wide choice of mainly local ales, including examples from Ridgeside and Kirkstall Breweries. Since my visit, a former function room in the yard has become a craft beer bar. On CAMRA's National Inventory of historic interiors; ambient music.

By boot, bike and boat: See page 74.

LIVERPOOL, MERSEYSIDE

Carvings and murals commissioned by an eccentric landlord

Peter Kavanagh's, 2-6 Egerton Street, L8 7LY.
Tel. 0151 709 3443.

From the street, stained glass windows give just a hint of the treasures within. This whitewashed hostelry, formerly called the Grapes, is at the end of a handsome terrace of Georgian

Some of the original murals in Peter Kavanagh's. Note the carved wooden heads at picture-rail height – there are 32 of them. The table-tops have special channels that direct spilt beer to the centre.

houses near the city's Anglican Cathedral. The interior is surprising: a series of rooms filled with time-faded murals and vintage paraphernalia and, on closer inspection, dotted with wooden carvings of faces, like miniature gargoyles. The oldest part, fitted out in 1929, consists of a servery set between front and rear rooms. The front Dickens Room is filled with Dickensian murals and the other, the Hogarth, has scenes of drinking and merrymaking: all are by Scottish artist Eric Robertson. Both rooms have stained and leaded windows by William English (including nautical and transport themes) and collections of wirelesses, chamber pots and musical instruments. A vintage radiogram has pride of place in the Dickens Room. Wood panelling and leather upholstered bench seating are other distinctive elements. Most of the wooden features, such as armrests, fire surrounds and panels, are brought to life by the array of carved heads. I counted thirty-two of them and many of the cartoon-like effigies are said to resemble the redoubtable Peter Kavanagh. Circular tables in the 'mural rooms' are also distinctive: designed by Mr Kavanagh,

they contain channels directing any spilt beer to grille-covered bowls, where cigarette ends could also be extinguished. The pub was extended in 1964 and 1977 and a large lounge created. This is full of old photos and prints and an assortment of memorabilia: a crocodile skin, three bicycles and numerous transistor radios, the latter suspended from ceilings and walls. The servery is similarly decorated. It has hand-pumps offering, on my visit, ales from Springhead, Greene King, Sharp's and Castle Rock.

Peter Kavanagh, born in 1873, was the licensee for fifty-three years until his death in 1950 and was responsible for the elaborate decoration. He was also a city councillor, successful business-man, artist and inventor. A faded photograph of him hangs in the lounge and, outside, his portrait graces the inn sign, where a brass plaque unveiled by the Lord Mayor in 1997 celebrates the centenary of his licence to sell liquor. There aren't many landlords so recognized sixty-five years after their passing. The pub has a community feel, being off the main tourist trail. No food served, though customers are welcome to bring their own. On CAMRA's National Inventory of historic interiors; ambient music; dog friendly.

By boot: **Get there by walking through historic Georgian streets from the Anglican Cathedral.** *By bike:* **Situated a few streets east of NCN Route 56, Liverpool-Chester via the Mersey Ferry.**

LLANTHONY, MONMOUTHSHIRE

A twelfth-century priory

Llanthony Priory Hotel, near Abergavenny, NP7 7NN. Tel. 01873 890487. www.llanthonyprioryhotel.co.uk

A ruined Augustinian priory at the foot of the Black Mountains is the setting for this diminutive cellar bar, popular with walkers and cyclists. The lofty ruins of the priory church date from the twelfth century and are majestic. Descend half-a-dozen steps and you are in a vaulted undercroft, formerly the prior's

Llanthony Priory Hotel in the Black Mountains. Entrance to the undercroft bar is through the open door on the left.

cellar, with benches and settles on a rough stone floor and a bar incorporated in one corner. I first discovered this place in the 1970s and have never forgotten it. It was a joy to return some forty years later, when researching this book, and discover that it had not changed at all, apart from an improved selection of ale and other fare. The bar is part of a small hotel within the priory, but this is understated to such an extent there is no name board or inn sign within the grounds. A Welsh theme prevails: three beers are served during the summer (one in winter) and on my visit these were Felinfoel Double Dragon, Celt Experience Native Storm and Three Beacons from Brecon Brewery, the latter very tasty for its strength (ABV 3%). There is a selection of whiskies, including a Welsh one. The lunchtime food menu is complemented with cakes, including bara brith and ice-cream. The setting, surrounded by hills, reminded me of Tintern Abbey but on a smaller scale and much more hidden. A serene and peaceful place, with no ambient music, television or other modern distractions. No dogs allowed; campsite nearby.

By boot: **The pub is just off the 177-mile Offa's Dyke National Trail, which follows the England-Wales border.** *By bike:* **On NCN Route 42 between Hay-on-Wye and Abergavenny.**

LONDON

Entries in the capital are alphabetical, by pub name. The full listing, by locality, can be found in the main index at the back. For notes on city-wide bicycle hire ('Boris bikes') see page 139.

Private drinking boxes
The Barley Mow, Marylebone
8 Dorset Street, W1U 6QW. Tel. 0207 487 4773.

Unusual for its two drinking boxes – the only ones to survive in London – where people could imbibe in privacy, untroubled by prying eyes. Of panelled wood construction and attached to one end of the bar counter, they enabled more important (or self important) individuals, such as upper class gentlemen, to drink separately from their servants. Pubs used to be divided into a number of rooms for the use of different classes of people, as seen from the three sets of entrance doors which once gave

One of the two private drinking boxes in the Barley Mow, Marylebone. Entry is via the door on the left.

access to separate bars. Division from your fellow human was enhanced further by these boxes, each still accessed by its own door. They contain bench seating, a coat hook and a length of bar counter where drinks can be ordered unseen by other customers. These rather cosy, late Victorian additions, are unsuitable for dining: my daughter and I had to retire to the main bar to enjoy lunch. The four-storey end-terrace building dates from the 1790s and a large sign outside declares it the 'oldest pub in Marylebone'. There are wood-panelled walls decorated with brewery mirrors, period prints and other memorabilia. A partially bare-board floor and a curving bar counter, fitted with brass standing rail and coat-hooks, complete the traditional look. A small snug to the rear has its own bar counter and a small lending library of books. The real ale selection on our visit included beers from West Berkshire, Mighty Oak, Wychwood, Truman's and Fuller's. Ambient music; dog friendly; closed Sunday.

By boot: **A short stroll from Baker Street.** *By bike:* **Bicycle hire docking stations in Paddington Street and Baker Street.**

Bar of the Black Friar, showing bas-reliefs of monks. Through the arches is a marble-lined grotto with further lavish decoration.

Ancient monastic survivor or an elaborate joke?
The Black Friar, **Blackfriars**
174 Queen Victoria Street, EC4V 4EG.
Tel: 0207 236 5474. www.nicholsonspubs.co.uk

This wedge-shaped building opposite Blackfriars Station houses the most surprising Art Nouveau pub interior in the country. No expense was spared on marble, brass or carved wood decoration in this celebration of the Dominican monastery that stood here until 1539. Its inhabitants were known as the Black Friars for the shade of their habits. Closer inspection of the decor – widely regarded as a work of art – reveals the designers had their tongues firmly in their cheeks. The brothers are depicted preparing feasts, carousing and enjoying the good things in life. A collection of irreverent inscriptions includes 'don't advertise it, tell a gossip', 'a good thing is soon snatched

up' and 'industry is ale'. The highlight is a marble-lined grotto resplendent with mosaic and gold leaf barrel-vaulted ceiling, alabaster bas-reliefs of monks, statuettes of imps and lamp brackets incorporating water (or ale) carrying brothers. Arched entrances to this inner sanctum have bronze effigies of well-fed friars. The main bar features large ecclesiastical murals captioned 'carols', 'tomorrow will be Friday' and 'Saturday afternoon'. Look for other details such as a stained-glass window of sunrise, a wood-case clock with attendant performing monkeys and, outside, fairy-tale and Aesop's Fables carvings and Worthington brewery plaques. The pub was once divided in two – a public bar and the more decorative lounge, with separate entrances.

Though dating from the 1870s, its exotic refurbishment took place thirty-five years later, under publican Alfred Pettitt, by Arts and Crafts architect H. Fuller-Clark, with embellishments by Henry Poole RA. An exterior statue of a rotund friar is more recent, probably from the 1980s. There are two marble-topped bar counters with hand-pumps dispensing, as common with other Nicholson's pubs, a pleasing variety of ales: examples from Acorn, Bays (Torbay), Bragdy Conwy and Moorhouses on my last visit. Food, including breakfast, is served. This place is popular with tourists from around the world, so get there early to best appreciate the decor and sign the visitors' book. Ambient music; outside seating at roadside.

By boot: **Why not plan your own pub crawl featuring the Olde Cheshire Cheese, Mitre (both page 92) and this pub, as they are within easy walking distance.** *By bike:* **Bicycle hire docking station in Tallis Street, Temple.** *By boat:* **Nearest River Bus pier is Blackfriars.**

Flower power: The Churchill Arms is covered in floral colour from pavement to chimney-pot. It is a regular winner of the London in Bloom competition.

London's most floral pub
The Churchill Arms, Kensington
119 Kensington Church Street, W8 7LN. Tel. 0207 727 4242. www.churchillarmskensington.co.uk

Passers-by stop and gaze, open-mouthed and coaches full of tourists slow down, cameras clicking, as they pass. The floral displays on this Victorian pub cover almost every inch of the exterior, extending from tubs on the pavement to baskets clinging to the roof. The horticultural hostelry is a regular winner of the London in Bloom competition. There are yet more plants inside – and the conservatory contains a waterfall complete with fish. It's the brainchild of landlord Gerry O'Brien, who has looked after this Fuller's house for more than thirty years and is known for his wicked sense of humour. 'Prince Edward pulled a pint two years ago when visiting as patron of the London Gardens Society and Alan Titchmarsh came to film for ITV. He re-potted one of my baskets that wasn't growing well,' he told the London *Evening Standard* in September 2014. He claims he has served more than two million pints of London Pride (other Fuller's real ales are also available). The bar is full of Churchillian memorabilia and other ephemera. A Thai menu is served in the butterfly themed conservatory. Two rows of rotating 'snob screens', designed to provide early customers with privacy from bar staff, are lined up along the bar counter. There are stained glass windows too, though you may not see them through the foliage. Dog friendly (not restaurant).

By boot: **Within walking distance of Kensington Gardens and Holland Park.** *By bike:* **Bicycle hire docking station in Vicarage Gate.**

Bizarrely restored 'forgotten' hotel
Clapton Hart, Clapton
231 Lower Clapton Road, E5 8EG. Tel. 020 8985 8124. http://claptonhart.com

You might be excused for thinking you had walked into a junk shop or the house of a bored DIY hobbyist. A rambling pub of ragged and bare brick walls, wood floors and peeling paint, this is the hostelry that time forgot. The frontage looks like it hasn't had a lick of paint in years and the four large rooms are filled with pre-owned furniture and other artefacts. Old pianos

On the site of a long closed hotel, the Clapton Hart has faded décor and memorabilia that could double as an Alfred Hitchcock film-set.

an inspired range of micro-brewery ales, usually including examples from East London Brewery. Thornbridge Jaipur, Otley Thai-Bo and APA, Tiny Rebel Fubar, Burning Sky Aurora, Volden Vim, Hackney Red and ELB White Night were available on my visit. The spacious garden is laid with shingle. Meals served; ambient music; dog friendly.

By bike, boot and boat: South-west of the River Lee Navigation and its towpath between Tottenham and Bow, which you leave at Lea Bridge Road.

masquerade as tables, there are veteran sofas and armchairs to sit on, sewing and weighing machines to admire and an impressive variety of fire surrounds. Two animal heads, a brewery mirror dedicated to Bass Brewers, a door and some Bakelite electrical sockets are among the items mounted around the walls. One ceiling is decorated with empty picture frames. In another room, a large museum cabinet is filled with pewter tankards, antique bottles, dolls and printers' blocks – and did I imagine that 1960s reel-to-reel tape machine left lying about?

On the site of the eighteenth century White Hart Hotel, rebuilt in the 1830s following a fire and again in the 1890s, it served in a number of guises, latterly as a nightclub, before closing in 2008. The present owners restored original features and left other parts untouched, to create the 'shabby chic' look, re-opening in 2012. In deference to the period feel, a weekly screening of cult films was being shown on VHS video at the time of writing (the season titled 'Stick it up your Betamax'). Even the DJs here use retro turntable decks rather than digital equipment. Candle-light, an assortment of chandeliers and various desk lamps provide lighting. Eight hand-pumps display

This cosy hideaway is named after its first licensee, George Colton Moor, who held it in 1849. When I first visited in early 2016, the pub had changed little since the 1950s and was full of carved

Closer inspection revealed this carved oak frieze in the bar of the Colton Arms to be part of an old wardrobe.

furniture rescued from local house sales. Drinks were rung on a pre-decimal cash register. A redecoration has swept much of that away, though added more beer choice and a trendy menu. The new owners have, however, retained some original features, including a large oak frieze in the bar - which started life as the front of a wardrobe. It is decorated with Bacchanalian hand maidens and nymphs riding chariots, while being serenaded by angels. Also still in place are a copper-topped bar counter with a frontage of sliced tree-trunks, and a serving hatch (in one of the two snugs) adapted from an old dresser. This is festooned with more carvings. Faux stone fire surrounds are other kitsch touches, as are cages housing a flock of artificial songbirds. On entering the upstairs toilet, I was momentarily fazed to discover its floor is an antique map of the locality. While seated, I mentally navigated my way around the squares and gardens of Victorian London. There are three hand-pumps, which were serving Truman's Knees-Up, Timothy Taylor Landlord and Fuller's London Pride. Patio garden; dog friendly; ambient music.

By boot and bike: **A visit to this pub makes a good excuse to explore the back streets of Kensington and Barons Court, home of Queen's Club tennis courts. Bicycle hire docking station in Greyhound Road, Hammersmith.**

Old factory with homemade furniture
Crate Brewery, Hackney Wick
The White Building, Unit 7, Queens Yard, E9 5EN. Tel. 07834 275687 http://cratebrewery.com

This former print works, situated beside the River Lea (or Lee) Navigation, near the Queen Elizabeth Olympic Park, is now part of East London's burgeoning micro-brewery scene. It opened as the home of Crate Brewery in 2012 and it's not only the cavernous industrial building that is unusual but its contents. Almost everything – furnishings, fittings, decorations and even the bar itself – is made from locally obtained recycled materials. The seating has been created from ladders and warehouse trolleys; tables from upturned crates, planks and

The Crate Brewery is a former print works beside the River Lea Navigation. Interior furnishings and decorations are made from recycled materials.

pallets. The bar-back is made of metal offcuts and lampshades are fashioned from old bedsprings. The bar counter (and, outside, the flower beds) have been built from railway sleepers. Mash tuns in the brewery are visible through large glass panels and you can see the house food speciality, pizza, being made in a kitchen behind the bar.

This is a trendy place: the clientele was predominantly young people in their twenties on my visit, and it was very busy on a bank holiday afternoon. DJs perform at weekends and at other times the ambient music is loud. There is outside seating beside the water. Though not exactly picturesque, the scene has post-industrial appeal, with narrow boats chugging by and nearby walls and bridges decorated with street art. I enjoyed a pint of Crate Best (ABV 4.3%) with its delicate hop flavours. There were five other beers on hand-pump, four of them brewed on-site, plus a guest (Welton's Hop Burst), real cider and a large selection of bottled beers, including Trappist. Brewery tours run twice a week and should be booked.

By boot and bike: **The River Lea Navigation offers an**

unbroken walking and cycling route from the Thames in London to rural Hertfordshire. Hackney Wick Overground and Stratford International Stations are within an easy walk. *By boat:* The Crate's own canal boat, the *Alfred Le Roy*, which is fitted with a bar and usually moored alongside the brewery, began offering regular cruises in spring 2016. Prior booking is advised.

One man's 'folly' – a monument in marble and mahogany
Crocker's Folly, St John's Wood
24 Aberdeen Place, St John's Wood, NW8 8JR. Tel. 020 7289 9898. www.crockersfolly.com

This ornate establishment, built in 1898 near Lord's Cricket Ground, was formerly the Crown Hotel but, since 1987, has taken its name from the remarkable Frank Crocker. The Victorian entrepreneur is said to have spent a fortune on it in

The bar of Crocker's Folly features stained glass, a stucco ceiling and gambolling cherubs on a gilt frieze. The grand saloon is even more lavish and is used mainly for dining.

the mistaken belief that the London terminus of the Great Central Railway would be constructed in St John's Wood. When it ended up a mile away in Marylebone, the despairing Crocker, approaching bankruptcy as a result, committed suicide from an upstairs window. In fact, the story is an urban myth, as work on the terminus was contemporaneous with the hotel and Frank died of natural causes in 1904. The sumptuous grand saloon, now the Marble Room with its marble faced walls, long bar-top (crafted from 50 types of marble), soaring pillars and ornate gilded ceiling, is now an upmarket restaurant, but the adjacent room has been preserved as a bar. While not quite as palatial, it is decorated with mirrors, stained glass windows, a stucco ceiling and gilt wall decoration featuring gambolling cherubs. A wood-case clock in the mahogany bar-back still bears the words 'Crown Hotel'. The Grade II* establishment reopened in 2014 following ten year's closure and a full restoration. There is no real ale: Fuller's London Pride was served from keg on my visit; draught Guinness and Peroni are also available. Bar snacks are available for those who don't wish to dine in more formal splendour next-door. Outside seating on front terrace; ambient music.

By boat: A few minutes' walk from the Regent's Canal and the beauty-spot of Little Venice. *By bike:* Bicycle hire docking station in Aberdeen Place. *By boat:* There are regular boat trips on Regent's Canal between Camden Lock and Little Venice.

Inner-city oasis – where you can ring for a beer
Dalston Eastern Curve Garden, Dalston
13 Dalston Lane, E8 3DF. www.dalstongarden.org

This hidden horticultural haven, almost opposite Dalston Junction Overground Station, is entered, Narnia style, through a doorway in a hoarding beside the Hackney Peace Carnival Mural. More open-air café than pub – though people of all ages treat it as their local – there aren't many cafés with such a commitment to ale and cider. The setting is a lavender-filled,

Lavender fills the foreground in this view of Dalston Eastern Curve Garden, reached through a doorway in some hoarding. Drinks (and cakes) are served from the lime green kiosk.

volunteer-run garden with trees and vegetable, herb and flower beds, carved out of abandoned railway land in 2010. It is the only venue I've visited where hops were growing rather than merely being dried decorations. Tables, chairs and benches, some made from recycled materials, are placed between the trees and there's a shady boardwalk. The main undercover area is a lofty but simple structure of wood, furnished with sofas and bean bags and decorated with paper lanterns. Service is from a box-like cabin with cakes, including chocolate orange and brownies, set on the counter alongside a Whitstable Bay Lager font. A brass bell is provided to call attention of the staff. Real ales (from bag-in-box containers) were Pale Ale and Foundation from East London Brewery, with Toast, a delicious craft beer made with surplus bread by Yorkshire's Hambleton Brewery, in bottles and three real ciders. Hot drinks are served as well as cakes; a wood oven is used to cook pizzas during weekly music nights in summer; or visitors can bring their own picnic (though not alcoholic drinks). A conservatory greenhouse, with

stove, provides indoor seating and is used for craft sessions. Children's' play area; dog friendly; accessible toilet. Opening hours are limited in winter and the site is subject to closure in bad weather.

By boot and boat: About twelve minutes' walk north of the Regent's Canal towpath, along Kingsland Road. *By bike:* There are bike racks outside the garden.

Secret garden hidden behind rooftops
The Faltering Fullback, Finsbury Park
19 Perth Road, N4 3HB. Tel. 0207 272 5834.
http://falteringfullback.com

The flowers and foliage covering the outside of this three-storey corner pub is impressive enough, but the real horticultural delight takes some seeking out. Make your way through the artefact-filled rooms to the rear, via the dimly-lit snug, and find the door to the garden. Entering an enclosed patio, it seems unpromising at first until you climb the first set of stairs. You

The multi-level garden of the Faltering Fullback, linked by wooden steps and covered walkways, is like a tree-house whose builder has run amok.

have discovered a delightful hideaway, its four levels linked by shady wooden steps and walkways. With the feel of a tropical jungle village and the look of a tree-house that has run amok, it has been cleverly hidden behind anonymous brick walls and rooftops. On my summer visit, the garden was filled with the scent of jasmine and the sound of trickling water features. There were flowers everywhere, above and below me, as well as bamboo and yucca contributing to the sub-tropical atmosphere. Seating areas are set at intervals on the various levels, the top tier being graced with a pagoda of sorts, decorated with exotic ornaments. It is a wonderful setting, particularly on a summer evening. Inside, the main horseshoe bar was busy with a young clientele, offering two cask ales, Fuller's London Pride and Truman's Swift, with bicycle, musical and aviation artefacts hanging from the ceiling. There is another, quieter bar too, and a large room at the rear where football and rugby is screened. As you will guess from the name, sport is an important feature of the pub, which was previously called the Sir Walter Scott. Thai food in the evenings; ambient music.

By boot and bike: **Five minutes' walk from Finsbury Park Station. The latter is starting point for a walk (or cycle) along the former railway line to Alexandra Palace, surprisingly leafy with views over North London.**

Lavender roof above the Gin Yard of the Four Thieves, Battersea. It provides a key ingredient in the pub's lavender-infused gin.

Lavender grown on roof for in-house distillery
The Four Thieves, Battersea
51 Lavender Gardens, SW11 1DJ. Tel. 0207 223 6927.
http://fourthieves.pub

It is hard to believe that lavender was once grown commercially on slopes surrounding bustling Clapham Junction Station. It is being grown once again, in a small way, on a rooftop in the gin-yard of this pub. The building was once a Victorian music-hall and later became the first Jongleurs comedy club. It was taken over by the Laine Brewing Company of Brighton, opening as a brewpub in 2014. As well as a microbrewery producing up to 40 casks per week, it houses a gin distillery. Both installations share a space visible through a glass partition. The site's tradition of live entertainment has been maintained. The split-level bar retains its Victorian feel, with varnished wooden flooring, bare brick walls, cast-iron ceiling supports and ornate (presumably original) ceramic tiling behind the bar counter. An eclectic selection of decor includes photographic studio lighting, modern art and enamel signs, with furniture a mixture of sofas, benches and antique wooden items. The paved gin-yard provides an outdoor drinking area, which also has a sheltered section imaginatively decorated with photos, prints and retro-style lighting, topped with the aforementioned lavender roof. There is also a separate snug. Eight hand-pumps are devoted to the company's ales, ranging from Light Ale (ABV 3.5%), through India Pale Ale (5%) to Chocolate Oatmeal Stout (5.7%). Some 70 gins were available on my visit, including two that are infused on the premises, not always using lavender. The food offering is strong on burgers, with traditional pub meals of pie, fish and chips and sharing platters (including vegetarian) available. Entertainment, including DJs, bands and comedians, is held in the adjacent Boat House. Ambient music; dog friendly until 8pm.

By boot: A few minutes' walk from the joggers' paradise that is Clapham Common. Ten minutes' from Clapham Junction. *By bike:* Bicycle hire docking station in Dorothy Road.

Bohemian boozer – often used as a film set
The George Tavern, Stepney
373 Commercial Road, E1 0LA. Tel. 0207 790 7335.
www.thegeorgetavern.co.uk

Almost every book about pubs will tell you about the galleried George Inn, in Southwark, mentioned in Shakespeare's *Henry VI* and frequented by Charles Dickens. Instead, I am focussing on another George, equally historic but less well-known, Stepney being somewhat off the tourist trail. The three-storey former coaching inn, with its early-nineteenth-century stucco facade, has been rescued through the efforts of one woman, artist Pauline Forster. She has been restoring it as a 'labour of love' for more than a decade and has been supported by celebrities from Georgia May Jagger to Kate Moss in her struggle to stave off residential development next door. Thanks to the pub's calendar of live music, this would sound its death-knell. In July 2016, it was announced that the George had won its Court of Appeal battle against the development, though the government is likely to seek to overturn this judgement. This Bohemian place has the lived-in look of a student house but oozing with charm. The interior, which includes a former Georgian theatre, is used by television and film companies making period dramas, but since it is also Pauline's home, the upper storeys are generally out-of-bounds. The bar, however, is open to all: a wood-panelled and floored room with recycled furniture, a stage and a ceiling supported by cast-iron pillars. Behind the bar are three superb ceramic tiled murals depicting the pub in various guises, including in the 1650s when it was known as the Halfway House. There has been a pub on the site for some 700 years. It was referenced by Geoffrey Chaucer in *The Reeve's Tale* written

The George Tavern in Stepney hosts variety shows and sing-alongs of the type that used to be common in London boozers.

in the 1380s; and known to diarist Samuel Pepys in the 1660s. To the side is a paved garden – formerly the main thoroughfare for horse-drawn coaches – now a backwater set with rustic furniture. In the eighteenth century, the inn was known for an adjoining botanic garden filled with exotic plants. The gardens may have gone but this is a pub where creativity and entertainment blossoms, including a monthly vintage variety show. This features acts such as a George Formby impersonator, drag *artistes* (the rumbustious Ruby Venezuela on my visit) and a piano sing-along, once a common feature of London pubs. There are also live bands, theatrical stagings and DJ nights. A stack of vinyl records behind the bar is ready for DJs who spurn the digital sound. One real ale, Sharp's Doom Bar, was available, with two Camden Town beers on keg, and free sandwiches on my visit. The gent's toilet makes a feature of its graffiti.

By bike: Bicycle hire docking station at Watney Market, Commercial Road.

Neon-lit Aladdin's Cave – on a trading estate

God's Own Junkyard (Rolling Scones Café), **Walthamstow**
Unit 12, Ravenswood Industrial Estate, Shernhall Street, E17
9HQ. Tel. 0208 509 0157 www.godsownjunkyard.co.uk

Europe's largest collection of neon signs is situated in a hidden corner of Walthamstow. One of them announces 'Sex, drugs and bacon rolls.' While not being an accurate description of the menu, it sums up the eccentricity of this place. At its heart is a licensed café (rather than a pub) but it's one of my favourite haunts – I make no excuse for including it. Many of the brightly lit advertising effects and works of 'electric art' were created for film and television and are often used for fashion shoots. They were built or collected by the 'Neon Man', the late Chris Bracey and the effect is psychedelic. Sofas and other seating is scattered among the exhibits, with a counter at the rear serving bottled ales from the Wild Card microbrewery (see below). There is no draught beer but coffee, tea and enticing cakes, along with a menu including hot dogs, burgers and toasted sandwiches. There is outside seating at the front and in a trendy yard, furnished with sheds and old signs. It's probably the most surreal place of

The counter at the Rolling Scones Café is surrounded by a dazzling collection of 'electric art.'

refreshment in the capital, usually open Friday through Sunday but check before travelling. Ambient music.

This compact estate has become something of a honey-pot, with the Wild Card microbrewery also open at weekends (Unit 7) and another, Four Pillars, newly established in summer 2016 (Unit 2). Mother's Ruin Gin Palace, serving liqueurs, occupies Unit 18.

By boot: The walk from Walthamstow Station takes about ten minutes, via the old village with its free Vestry House Museum. Afterwards, a local pub crawl could include the nearby Nag's Head; Mirth, Marvel and Maud (page 89) and Ye Olde Rose and Crown theatre pub. *By bike:* Waltham Forest, including Walthamstow Village, has London's first 'Mini Holland' scheme, including some 20mph zones, which aims to encourage cycling.

Members of the Handlebar Club at its previous home, the Windsor Castle. The club's monthly meetings, and its paraphernalia, relocated to the Heron in 2016.

Meeting place of the Handlebar Club
The Heron, Paddington
Norfolk Crescent, W2 2DN. Tel. 020 7724 8463.

Founded in 1947, the Handlebar Club is devoted to the owners of handlebar moustaches world-wide. For ten years, it met in the Windsor Castle off the Edgware Road, an exotic place, decorated with royal and sporting memorabilia, along with artefacts ranging from a miniature Edwardian paddle-steamer to a Toby jug collection. The hostelry's sudden closure in 2016 led to the club's transfer to the above venue, which may or may not turn out to be a permanent residency. Its gatherings take place from 8pm on the first Friday of each month. Discussions cover the finer points of facial hair curling and waxing; the latest on the British Beard and Moustache Championships, as well as equally important topics such as pubs, beer and cricket. They are a sociable bunch, but if you find the conversation waning or you're there on a non-meeting day, there is the pub to admire. Though a modern, flat-roofed building, inside it is wood-panelled and traditional, with a cosy atmosphere and plenty of memorabilia. This ranges from the above-mentioned

Toby jugs to a gallery of handlebar portraits on the ceiling as well as walls; wood-case clocks and tables bearing engraved club plaques. There is a Thai restaurant downstairs and this cuisine is also served in the bar. An ornate, wooden coat-of-arms above the fireplace is said to have been rescued from a decommissioned court room. Three real ales, including Wadworth's 6X and Sharp's Doom Bar, plus a range of craft beers. Beer garden; ambient music.

By bike: Bicycle hire docking station in Nutford Place. *By boat:* Visitor moorings at Paddington Basin on the Grand Union Canal (about ten minutes' walk).

The pub with 371 owners
The Ivy House (formerly Newlands Tavern), Nunhead
40 Stuart Road, SE15 3BE. Tel. 020 7277 8233.
www.ivyhousenunhead.com

A price list framed beside the bar brings back happy memories: London Mild at 1/11d a pint (less than 10p in today's money),

A vintage price list still has pride of place at the Ivy House, Nunhead. It was London's first community-run pub.

Ben Truman 1/8d a bottle, Eagle Stout just 1/4d. Varnished wall panelling in the multi-roomed hostelry is embossed with gilt lettering announcing Burton Brewed Bitter and Trubrown Ale. This three-storey Improved Public House, built in the 1930s as the bright future of hospitality, belonged to London brewer Truman but closed in 2012, its future destined to be a residential one. Cue dedicated local campaigners and CAMRA, who fought the developers and won, creating the capital's first community owned pub. It was also Britain's first to be listed as an Asset of Community Value and boasts 371 shareholders, most of them also customers. It sells a range of real ales and ciders – seven on my visit – including Swift, an ale from the born-again Truman's Brewery. Rekindling its time on the 1970s pub rock circuit, when it hosted musicians such as Dr Feelgood, Jeff Beck and Ian Drury, the Ivy stages regular live jazz and other bands on a curtained stage. There are other events for all ages and a wonderful community atmosphere – heartening for anyone concerned about the long-term future of pubs. Food served; dog friendly; paved garden.

By boot: The 50-mile Green Chain Walk from Thamesmead ends at nearby Nunhead Cemetery. A walk around this Victorian 'Valhalla', created by the London Necropolis Company in the nineteenth century, is fascinating.

Cradle of coffee drinking – with mahogany screens
Jamaica Wine House, Cornhill
St Michael's Alley, Cornhill, EC3V 9DS.
Tel. 020 7929 6972. www.shepherdneame.co.uk

A giant iron lantern more than 4 feet high is an unusual sight above the door. The 'jam pot,' as it's affectionately known, is significant not for lighting but for its place in the history of coffee drinking. A blue plaque records that it stands on the site of London's first coffee house, Pasqua Rosée's, dating from 1652. Coffee houses became fashionable places in which to conduct business and exchange news and ideas – Lloyd's of London was established in one – this one was used by slave traders and West India Company merchants. Rosée created the establishment in collaboration with a merchant who traded with Turkey: it was later known as the Turk's Head. According to the Museum of London, there is evidence that slaves were advertised for sale, as

The Jamaica Wine House, dating from 1652, was London's first coffee house and early customers included slave traders.

were rewards for the recapture of runaways. Diarist Samuel Pepys was a customer. The current building is of sandstone and brick and was designed by Banister Fletcher in 1885. A remarkable interior is partially divided into four drinking areas by three mahogany screens, at right angles to a long bar counter. The ceiling decoration is varied, one part boasting ornate enamelled metal panels in wood frames. It is set in one of a number of narrow alleyways and courtyards off Cornhill, a few minutes from the Bank of England. Now a Shepherd Neame house, it serves a selection of the Kent brewer's ales. Closed at weekends. Food served; wine bar downstairs.

By boot: **Essential refreshment stop on any exploration of the Square Mile. Possibly on one of the themed walking tours that are operated by companies such as London Walks.** *By bike:* **Bicycle hire docking station at Bank of England Museum.**

Containing a classical statue and wash-stand reminiscent of a cathedral font, the ladies' toilet in the Knights Templar.

Luxurious toilet in a bank vault
The Knights Templar, Chancery Lane
95 Chancery Lane, WC2A 1DT. Tel. 0207 831 2660.
www.jdwetherspoon.com

I discovered this plush pub's convenience on a guided London Loo Tour advertised as 'not the bog-standard London experience'. I spent an amusing ninety minutes walking around Bloomsbury with a female guide who carried a sink plunger, being regaled with stories of pioneering plumbing and characters such as the redoubtable Thomas Crapper. We visited the gents' in Holborn's Princess Louise pub, which is a wonderfully restored Victorian gin palace, but the ladies' toilet on the lower floor of this J.D. Wetherspoon pub was the highlight *des toilettes*. With cast iron columns, full length mirrors, sofas, mosaic tiling, mood lighting, a *faux* classical statue and wash-stand akin to a cathedral font, it is the ultimate 'loo with a view'. One customer told *Wetherspoon News* 'I feel like bringing my pint down and hanging out down there among it all.' The gents', by comparison, is quite ordinary. The building,

dating from 1865, is the former Union Bank – the ladies' was once a vault – while the spacious bar contains fluted columns, marble arches, mahogany doors and gilt-framed windows. A wide range of real ales was available and meals are served all day.

By boot: **Details on the Bloomsbury London Loo Tour, a lavatory themed walking tour, from www.lootours.com.** *By bike:* **Bicycle hire docking station in Chancery Lane (Breams Buildings).**

Cinema with 'hall of mirrors'
Mirth, Marvel and Maud, Walthamstow
186 Hoe Street, E17 4QH. Tel. 0208 520 8636.
http://mirthmarvelandmaud.com

Opened in 2015, in a 1930s, Moorish-style cinema, this pub-restaurant is the first stage of what it is hoped will be a full

The Spanish Baroque foyer of Mirth, Marvel and Maud. When a concert hall, the venue hosted top acts such as the Beatles and Buddy Holly.

revival of this entertainment venue. The roll-call of past performers includes Buddy Holly, the Rolling Stones, the Beatles and James Brown, among other bands of the 1950s-60s, so the place is regarded with great affection. The interior decoration, in Spanish Baroque, makes for a grand foyer that extends upstairs to a balcony promenade with a vaulted ceiling. The 'hall of mirrors' is hung with mirrors of all shapes and sizes along its vast length, with others adding sparkle to the foyer. A modern bar counter is situated at lower ground level and the stand-alone 'box office' sells cocktails. Five lesser-seen real ales, including examples from Great Heck, Outlaw, Ticketybrew of Stalybridge and several specially brewed by Volden of Croydon, were on hand-pump; there were craft beers too. Meals are served in the upstairs dining area. The 1000-seat auditorium was closed when I visited but there are ambitions for its restoration. Opened as the second establishment in the Granada chain in 1930, the cinema changed ownership several times, to Cannon, MGM, ABC and EMD, before screenings ceased in 2003. It was then boarded up for thirteen years and the Grade II* listed structure lay dormant until its 2014 acquisition by Antic Pub Company. Outside seating; ambient music; events. Opens late afternoon Monday-Friday. A separate pub, The Victoria, occupies the former cinema restaurant next door.

By boot: A self-guided local walking tour could include God's Own Junkyard and Wild Card microbrewery (page 86), and some noteworthy pubs, such as the Nag's Head and Ye Olde Rose and Crown theatre pub.

Private jetty from where the Pilgrim Fathers sailed
The Mayflower, Rotherhithe
117 Rotherhithe Street, SE16 4NF.
Tel. 0207 237 4088. www.mayflowerpub.co.uk

A sign on the pub's covered jetty, built on piles above the restless Thames waters, warns outdoor drinkers: 'Feet and belongings may get wet at high tide.' When it is excessively high the area has to be closed to prevent customers getting soaked. A well-thumbed book of tide tables is kept behind the bar for this purpose. The river can be seen and heard through the planking – and boats pass by every few minutes. A Union Jack and the Stars and Stripes flutter from the timbers, marking an historic event linking two continents. In 1620, the Pilgrim Fathers' ship *Mayflower* set sail from this spot on the first stage of her journey to the New World. She returned eight months later to rot away when the captain, Christopher Jones, died after a short illness. He lies buried, with a fitting monument, in the churchyard opposite. The pub, originally the Ship, was renamed the Spreadeagle & Crown following a seventeenth-century rebuild, changing to today's title following a restoration in the late 1950s. Once at the heart of London's docks, with warehouses either side, it was busy with seamen. It was the only pub in London that also served as a post office – specially for these visiting sailors – but sadly the postal service ceased long ago. A candle-lit, wood-beamed interior conveys the atmosphere of a maritime tavern. The bar has bench seating and there is a separate snug, with old local photos, while upstairs is

The River Thames seen from the jetty of the Mayflower, Rotherhithe. A sign at the pub advises 'feet and belongings may get wet at high tide.'

a full-service restaurant with river views. Downstairs was busy (also mainly with diners) when I visited on a midweek September evening and there were six real ales available – some from the pub owner Greene King's stable but also including Black Sheep My Generation, Dark Star Hophead and Hardy & Hanson's Mayflower Scurvy Ale. The menu, served all day, is wide ranging and includes an annual Thanksgiving menu.

By boot: The pub is on the Thames Path between Bermondsey and Deptford. *By bike:* On the Tower Bridge to Greenwich section of NCN Route 4.

A working 'what the butler saw' and penny arcade delights
The Nag's Head, Belgravia
53 Kinnerton Street, SW1X 8ED. Tel. 0207 235 1135.

This diminutive hostelry, nestling among mews flats away from the hubbub of Knightsbridge, is a hidden gem on the Duke of Westminster's estate. It is reminiscent of a cottage museum, filled with knick-knacks that include everything from vintage wirelesses and penny arcade machines to Toby jugs, boots, walking sticks and military insignia. Every square inch of the

wood-panelled walls – and several ceilings – are lined with photographs and ephemera; even the toilet doors sport jokey wood cameos for each gender. The highlight is a veteran 'what the butler saw' machine which displays an illuminated show of monochrome beauties from the Edwardian era. To work it you insert an old penny, obtained from the bar in exchange for a donation to a local charity. There are two bars, one upstairs with an unusually low bar counter and the other, with a flagstone floor, downstairs. Both have bench seating and coal-fired ranges in ornate fireplaces. But it is the landlord who makes this place, keeping an ever-watchful eye and maintaining standards which include a strict 'no mobile phone' rule. Five hand-pumps dispense a range of Adnams beers that included Lighthouse and Ghost Ship on my visit. Ambient music; food served; outside seating beside street.

By bike: Bicycle hire docking station in Seville Street (Knightsbridge end).

Vintage one-armed bandits at the Nag's Head. There is also an old 'what the butler saw' still using pre-decimal pennies.

Historic tavern with resident parrot
Olde Cheshire Cheese, Fleet Street
145 Fleet Street, EC4A 2BU. Tel. 0207 353 6170.

Hidden in an alley off Fleet Street, this is a survivor from a bygone age. Wood-panelled walls are hung with fading portraits, there are narrow corridors, hard bench seats, sawdust-scattered wood floors, pewter tankards and, in winter, coal fires glowing in blackened hearths. This was lexicographer Samuel – 'When a man is tired of London he is tired of life' – Johnson's local. Charles Dickens mentions it in *A Tale of Two Cities*; James Boswell, Thackeray and Conan Doyle also called here for glasses of sherry or pints of porter. A chop house in the seventeenth century, it was rebuilt after the Great Fire of 1666. The oldest rooms are the two at the front: the left-hand 'chop room' is an unspoilt dining area in the style of old London taverns, while the right-hand bar bears the lettering 'Gentlemen only served in this bar' (no longer true of course). It is enhanced by a wood-case clock, sliding serving hatch and a fireplace that seems extravagant for the compact room. Descending a narrow staircase takes you to the vault, where there is a more recent cellar bar while, upstairs, is the Johnson Bar and further rooms for dining or functions.

The pub has long had a resident parrot. The present incumbent is Coco but a predecessor, a talkative African Grey named Polly, lived there for forty years. Among her repertoire, she could imitate a popping cork. News of her death in 1926 was reported by the BBC and newspapers worldwide. The 'Cheese' has always been popular: a newspaper cutting in the bar, dated 1815, states 'So great is the afflux of diners that many persons find it convenient to order their dinner an hour or two beforehand ... on returning [it] is instantly served up smoking, and their porter foaming.' Beers are from Samuel Smith's range and meals are served. On CAMRA's National Inventory of historic interiors.

By boot: You can plan your own pub crawl featuring the **Black Friar (page 78), Mitre (below) and this pub as they are within walking distance.** *By bike:* Bicycle hire docking station in Bouverie Street.

Ye Olde Cheshire Cheese was frequented by Charles Dickens, Samuel Johnson and Conan Doyle, among others. Today, it is home to Coco, the latest in a long line of parrots.

Queen Elizabeth I's cherry tree
Ye Olde Mitre, Ely Place
1 Ely Court, Ely Place, EC1N 6SJ. Tel. 020 7405 4751.
http://yeoldemitreholborn.co.uk

Possibly the capital's most successfully hidden pub, it is accessed from a narrow passageway between Hatton Garden and Ely Place. One writer described finding the alleyway entrance, near a lamp-post, as 'like stumbling across Narnia.' Said to have been founded in the sixteenth century for the servants of the Bishop of Ely, being adjacent to his great palace (now demolished), the land it stands upon passed to the Crown in the eighteenth. It remains in this noble ownership and is therefore

Ye Olde Mitre is hidden in an alleyway, on Crown land, making it outside the jurisdiction of the City of London.

outside the jurisdiction of the City of London. The petrified remains of a cherry tree which Queen Elizabeth I is said to have danced around with her Lord Chancellor and favourite gentleman, Sir Christopher Hatton, is preserved behind glass in a corner of the front bar. A plaque above states 'Built by Bishop Goodrich in 1546. The Cherry Tree marks the boundary between the Bishop's garden and the part leased to Sir Christopher Hatton.' The pub's attractive exterior is glazed with small panes. Its interior, with *faux* Tudor panelling, dates from circa 1930 and is on CAMRA's National Inventory of historic interiors. There are two ground floor bar rooms, either side of a central servery, the rear one boasting a lantern roof and cosy snug with bench seating (marked 'Ye Closet'). As you would expect from an historic hostelry that has won numerous CAMRA awards, it is invariably busy, so get there early for a seat. The gents' toilet is accessed from outside. Six hand-pumps dispense a changing selection of cask ales and a cider. On my visit the guests were Dark Star Hophead and Castle Rock Mild. Being a Fuller's pub, this London brewer's ales always feature – London Pride, Oliver's Island and Gale's Seafarers on this

occasion. Food is home-made bar snacks – no chips. Closed at weekends.

By boot: You can plan your own pub crawl featuring the Black Friar (page 78), Olde Cheshire Cheese (page 92) and this pub as they are within walking distance. *By bike:* Bicycle hire docking station in Hatton Garden.

The largest station pub, in a parcels office
The Parcel Yard, King's Cross
King's Cross Station, N1C 4AH. Tel. 020 7713 7258.
www.parcelyard.co.uk

Ignore Harry Potter's luggage trolley half buried in the wall of 'Platform 9¾' – and its queue of camera-toting tourists – if you want to discover the station's best kept secret. The Parcel Yard is unexpectedly cavernous, reached via a flight of stairs (and lift) near the real platform nine. Occupying the 10,000-square foot, Grade I-listed former Great Northern Railway parcels office – part of the original terminus of 1852 – it became 'the largest station pub in the country' (according to owner Fuller's) on opening in 2012. The central feature is a bright, double-height atrium, with glazed skylights and triangular roof trusses. The upper floors were once suspended from these, avoiding the need for supporting columns. This enabled horse-drawn carts to enter and turn without unhitching. There are many other original features in the labyrinthine pub, which is decorated with railway artefacts, posters, original artwork – and parcel trolleys. I also liked the wooden lifting seats, the games room and 'stationmaster's office', being function rooms off a corridor. Bar counters on two floors each have six hand-pumps, serving the full range of Fuller's ales – such as London Pride and ESB, plus guest ales. Meals are served all day, including breakfast; screens give train departure information. If refreshments in railway buildings interest you, see our sister volume *Unusual Railway Pubs* (Halsgrove). Ambient music; 'outside' terrace.

By boot and bike: The Regent's Canal is nearby, its towpath providing a traffic-free route between Paddington

This composite image, using a dozen separate photographs, conveys the size of the double-height atrium in the Parcel Yard, King's Cross. When originally built, the upper floors were suspended from roof trusses, so horses and carts could turn around without unhitching.

and Limehouse. Bicycle hire docking station in Goods Way. *By boat:* Mooring is at a premium on the canal and generally restricted to double mooring to allow boats to pass. Visitor moorings are proposed between York Way and Caledonian Road.

A 'mini Red Lion' and an annual panto
The Red Lion, Isleworth
92-94 Linkfield Road, TW7 6QJ. Tel. 020 8560 1457.
www.red-lion.info

A handsome local in an otherwise ordinary suburban street. A hub of the local community, its customers are aged from four to ninety-four. In a yard at the back is a brick-built old stable

which is used during beer festivals (usually August, with others planned). This annex is known to staff and locals variously as the 'cave', the 'dungeon' or simply the 'ale house'. From the outside, it looks like a mini version of the pub, carrying a name board and vintage Courage lamp. Unfurnished, lined with pump-clips and with casks set against one wall, most of the time it is simply a store room – but comes into its own during the said events. There's a simple covered shelter outside: seating used to take the form of two old sofas, since replaced by a picnic bench. The landlord plans to open a micro-brewery in part of the building. The pub proper has two bars, a public bar and lounge, the latter with an adjoining room, complete with stage, used for live music and a pantomime. Performed annually by the Hiss & Boo Pantomime Company, whose cast is made up of regulars. They cut their teeth with 'A Lad in Bar', a satirical take on 'Aladdin', in 1997. The risqué 'Whip Dickington' followed in 2000. There is also a weekly jazz night and other events. Nine real ales were on hand-pump (more during festivals), including Twickenham Naked Ladies (ABV 4.4%) on my visit, plus three real ciders. Garden; dog friendly.

The 'little Red Lion', at the rear of the Isleworth pub of the same name, in March 2014. Inside, it is set up for a beer festival.

By boot: The River Thames at Isleworth Ait is within walking distance, though the Thames Path National Trail uses the opposite bank.

Four nymphs provide ethereal illumination
The Salisbury, Covent Garden
90 St Martin's Lane, WC2N 4AP. Tel. 020 7836 5863.
www.taylor-walker.co.uk

An orgy of engraved glass, mirrors and carved mahogany, this is one of London's finest examples of late Victorian pub design. Set in a prime location in the heart of Theatreland, it is always busy. Actors are among the clientele, past customers having included Richard Burton, Sir Michael Caine, Sir John Mills and Sir Dirk Bogarde, whose photos adorn the snug. Dating from 1898 it is named for the Marquess of Salisbury, who was thrice Prime Minister. Its four ornate, Art Nouveau lamps are unique features, depicting a female hunter – possibly based on the Greek goddess Artemis – in copper, complete with dog and a quiverful of arrows. Each exquisite statuette, set at regular intervals behind semi-circular bench seats, incorporates three floral lights on stalks 'blooming' above. There are more impressive light fittings suspended behind the original island bar counter, which is partly topped with white marble and has a stunning bar-back. The pub is still sub-divided, with a separate dining area and snug bar, the latter complete with

One of the four Art Nouveau 'lady lamps' that are a highlight of the ornate Salisbury in Covent Garden. The background has been digitally removed for clarity.

fireplace, glazed screen and its own entrance. There was a selection of eight ales on my visit, including Purity Mad Goose, Timothy Taylor Landlord, Harvey's Best and St Austell Tribute. Meals are served all day. Ambient music.

By bike: Bicycle hire docking station in William IV Street, Strand.

Replica of the detective's study
Sherlock Holmes, St James's
10 Northumberland Street, WC2N 5DB. Tel. 020 7930 2644. www.sherlockholmes-stjames.co.uk

For a fictional detective, Sherlock Holmes has surprising number of tangible properties in the capital. His 'home', 221B Baker Street, can be found in said street and is a museum, while his statue stands beside Baker Street Station. This pub contains the most surprising item of all: a full-size replica of his supposed study, crammed with artefacts, along with cabinets of memorabilia including pipes, magnifying glasses, pocket watches and letters. The Victorian building, originally the

The author stands, a pint of Sherlock Ale in hand, in front of Sherlock Holmes's study. This has been a feature of the eponymous pub since 1957.

Northumberland Hotel before becoming the Northumberland Arms pub, featured in Conan Doyle's story *The Noble Bachelor*, published in 1892 and, plausibly, *The Hound of the Baskervilles* (1901). Downstairs is a large bar with a central counter and a few items, including a bust of dog Toby used by the detective, but the study is protected behind glass screens upstairs. The area is set aside for diners. Look for details such as the set of chemicals and the famous cape and deerstalker hat, while a wax replica of the detective himself includes a bullet hole in his head. Not as macabre as it looks, enthusiasts will know it's an effigy; a ruse in one of Conan Doyle's stories. A brass plaque records that the study is the work of Jack Thorne (1916-2001) who also made one for the 1951 Festival of Britain. It has been in the pub since 1957 and is maintained by the Sherlock Holmes Society of London. Photographs and posters from various film and television versions also decorate the building. Six real ales were available, all from the Greene King stable, including Sherlock Ale (a house version of Morland's Original, ABV 4.1%) and Watson's Gold (4.1%). I luncheoned on Dr Watson's Sunday roast (available every day – another unusual feature) accompanied by customers of varying nationalities. The eccentric sleuth is evidently still revered around the globe: also, his 'birthday' is celebrated here each January. Ambient music; seating outside at front and on first floor terrace.

By boot: Trafalgar Square and the River Thames, with a footbridge to the South Bank, are a few minutes' walk. *By bike:* Bicycle hire docking station off the Strand (Craven Street). *By boat:* Riverboat services to/from Embankment Pier, six minutes' walk.

Was there a prison beneath this old gin palace?
Viaduct Tavern, Newgate Street
126 Newgate Street, EC1A 7AA. Tel. 020 7600 1863.
www.viaducttavern.co.uk

This corner pub, named in honour of Holborn Viaduct, is set opposite the Central Criminal Courts (Old Bailey) in an area where the most notorious prisons were once located and public executions drew huge crowds. Its melodramatic atmosphere is probably down to the fact it was once an ornate gin palace. The Viaduct has been reduced from its multi-roomed beginnings, *circa* 1870, to one big room, albeit a space with gilded cut glass panels and high, decorative ceiling. These are upstaged by three large portraits of maidens, said to represent agriculture, commerce, science and the arts. One displays a bullet or bayonet hole, possibly from an over-zealous WWI soldier. Behind the bar counter is an ornate glazed office where money was exchanged for gin tokens (counterfeit coins were a problem and staff were not trusted to handle money). What makes this place most unusual, however is below rather than above ground level. If you ask behind the bar and staff aren't too busy, they will

Some claim these cellars, in the Viaduct Tavern, were used as prison cells. Opposite is the site of Newgate Prison, where the Central Criminal Courts (Old Bailey) now stands.

happily show you the 'prison cells'. I was given an impromptu tour by an enthusiastic employee. Descending steep steps, I was led into the cellar where there are damp, dingy rooms said once to house prisoners. They did not belong to Newgate Prison, which was opposite but, I was told, were possibly part of Giltspur Street Compter (cells for debtors). If these *were* cells they were among the capital's smallest – unlit and overcrowded. Geoff Brandwood, author of *Britain's Best Real Heritage Pubs*, debunks the theory: 'It [the debtors' prison] was on a different site and closed in 1853.' I was also told the Post Office's former automated underground railway ran a few feet away. The pub is reputedly haunted, several mediums having sensed something in the cellars, according to author Richard Jones (*Walking Haunted London,* New Holland 1999, 29). One manager was, apparently, trapped by a ghost staff called Fred. The Viaduct belongs to London brewer Fuller's and four of the company's brews, including London Pride, Wild River and Oliver's Island, were served on my visit. As a nod to its gin palace past, many branded gins are available. There is a varied menu including traditional pub snacks. Closed at weekends.

By boot: **For more history on this fascinating area, including prisons and ghosts, try one of the guided walks from London Walks – www.walks.com.** *By bike:* **Bicycle hire docking station on Snow Hill.**

The White Cross at Richmond. The River Thames has flooded the road (foreground) but customers still manage to use the garden. During very high tides the steps to the pub are the only access.

River blocks entrance at high tide
The White Cross, Richmond
Riverside (off Water Lane), TW9 1TH.
Tel. 020 8940 6844. http://thewhitecrossrichmond.com

Usually situated beside the River Thames, on very high tides this pub appears to be in it. Though the building does not flood, water laps against the walls and one of the entrances becomes inaccessible. At these times look for the doorway with the sign reading 'entrance at high tide.' Many an unwary motorist has returned to their parked car to find it partially submerged outside. Inside, the White Cross has an unusual feature: a window in the bar has a real fire blazing beneath it. Work out where the flue goes to reach the chimney – it is a mystery. This curious arrangement allows customers a river view while sitting beside the fire (there's another such window upstairs, I was told). The Palladian-style building dates from the 1830s and stands on the site of a medieval house of the Observant Friars, taking its name from their badge and commemorated by a glass panel. There is a patio beer garden with river views and a bar at busy times. Real ale is from Young's and Wells and meals are served all day. Dog friendly.

By boot: **On the 184-mile Thames Path National Trail, which facilitates local walks to Kew Gardens, Ham House etc.** *By bike:* **This section of the Thames Path is perfect for cycling. The Tamsin Trail provides an almost traffic-free circuit of nearby Richmond Park, linking with NCN Route 4.** *By boat:* **River trips to Ham House and Hampton Court operate from Richmond Pier during the season. Details from Turks, tel. 020 8546 2434, www.turks.co.uk.**

Original music hall pub
Wilton's Music Hall (Mahogany Bar), Whitechapel
1 Graces Alley, off Brick Lane, E1 8JB.
Tel. 0207 702 2789. www.wiltons.org.uk

London's only intact survivor of the Grand Music Hall era, Wilton's is a very special place. It started life as an alehouse *circa* 1690. John Wilton bought the Prince of Denmark pub, then known as the Mahogany Bar, in the early 1850s, later purchasing adjoining houses and building an auditorium across the back yards. His music hall opened in 1859 with popular performers such as Champagne Charlie (George Leybourne) and Arthur Lloyd on the bill. From 1888-1950 it became a Methodist mission, falling into dereliction and decay thereafter. Campaigns by Spike Milligan and Sir John Betjeman saved the building from demolition and restoration to a music hall began in 1997. A fundraising campaign between 2012-15 has enabled its repair and secured its Grade II-listed structure. There is a regular programme of theatre and other performances. The front-of-house focal point is once again the Mahogany Bar. Though the elaborate fittings that gave this its name are long gone, it is a lively place with bare boards and plaster walls. Decorated with old posters and an illuminated 'Wilton's' sign. A curved, wood-topped bar counter is decorated with ornate plasterwork and has three hand-pumps serving, on my visit, East London Brewing Pale Ale, Wapping (Hockey Club) Gold and Adnams Prop Hop. There is an upright piano and regular live music, often from the swing era. On show days there is a snack menu, with full meals available from the cocktail bar upstairs. When the rest of the music hall is open, it is possible to walk across the corridor to an historical exhibition in the John Wilton Room. There is a cinema room and Champagne Charlie Room upstairs and tours of the building are organized weekly. Closed Sunday; ambient music.

By boot: **A few minutes' walk from the Tower of London and St Katharine's Dock. Nearest Underground is Tower Hill.** *By bike:* **Bicycle hire docking station in Dock Street.**

LYDIATE, MERSEYSIDE

Built around an oak tree – Lancashire's oldest inn
The Scotch Piper, Southport Road, L31 4HD.
www.admiraltaverns.co.uk

To walk into this thatched hostelry is to step back in time. Rough-hewn oak beams rise from a rendered floor, there is the gentle hum of conversation and a fire crackles in the small but busy bar, filling the place with the scent of wood-smoke. There are no twenty-first century distractions such as background music, television, gaming machines or dining to disturb the time-honoured business of drinking and conversing. Even the toilets are relegated to a separate outbuilding. The glazed servery, with its simple counter, is in the corner of the public bar, the rest of which is taken up with bench seating, rustic wooden furniture and a fireplace. The landlord pointed out a broad cruck timber rising from the floor near the fire and explained that this is reputedly the oak around which the

The Mahogany Bar at Wilton's, London's last Grand Music Hall.

The Scotch Piper at Lydiate is the oldest inn in Lancashire. Its name recalls a romantic story concerning the innkeeper's daughter.

original beer house was built. Two other rooms are set off a wood-beamed corridor, one of which has a dartboard and the other, a lounge, has a carpet as a small concession to modernity. This room was once a barn for animals and later became the landlady's living room. Beer was once fetched directly from the cellar but there are now three hand-pumps, serving Liverpool Craft IPA, Beartown Kodiak Gold and the house ale, Piper's 1320 from Marston's, on my visit.

A date of AD 1320 shown on the exterior is probably optimistic; tree-ring dating carried out in 1985 indicated structural timbers dating from circa 1450. The building, which is a three-bay cruck frame construction encased in brick, probably became an inn somewhat later when it was called the Royal Oak. The current name originates from a story that an injured piper from the 1745 Jacobite rebellion took refuge here and married the innkeeper's daughter. Cock-fighting took place during the lordship of Francis Anderton, another Jacobite rebel who was pardoned by the king on condition he retired to 'a quiet country life' in 1729. The pub was taken over by Burtonwood in 1945 and, from 1961 to 2014 was run by the same family. It is the venue for a popular biker meet on Wednesday evenings, when up to 500 attend and, in summer, a barbeque and tea shed provide refreshments. Garden; dog

friendly. Reopening in 2017 following restoration after a fire in late 2016.

By boat and bike: Situated north of bridge 17A on the Leeds & Liverpool Canal (note you can only exit the towpath on the east side of the bridge). Cyclists can use the Trans Pennine Trail (NCN Route 62) on the former Cheshire Lines track bed, to the site of Lydiate Station.

MANCHESTER, GREATER MANCHESTER

Murals of a massacre – and more than 300 whiskies
The Britons Protection, 50 Great Bridgewater Street, M1 5LE. Tel. 0161 236 5895.

Great Bridgewater Street is fortunate in having two classic pubs (see also Peveril of the Peak). Thanks to a remodelling in the 1930s and caring proprietors since then, this one has a wonderful array of period features, including ornately tiled walls and floors, moulded ceilings, upholstered bench seating, interior leaded windows, decorative fire surrounds and wooden

Some of the murals depicting the 1819 Peterloo Massacre, in the Britons Protection, Manchester.

serving hatches. In the front public bar is a heated foot-rail, while the rear snug retains bell pushes that customers once used to order drinks. Even the toilets are of interest, the gents boasting large urinals from the 1930s and the ladies a double-hinged saloon-type door. Of particular interest is a series of four murals depicting the Peterloo Massacre that happened in the city in 1819. Fifteen people were killed when armed cavalry charged a huge crowd of protestors. Should viewing these prove distressing, there are 330 bottles of different malt whiskies lined up behind the bar to perk you up. The barman apologized as 'there should be 360 but we're having difficulty sourcing some.' There were also five cask ales, including several from Moorhouses, and Cottage Nemesis, on my visit. The unusual pub name dates from its use by army recruiters during the Napoleonic wars – it was in business as early as 1811. Food served, including a choice of pies. Patio beer garden.

By boot: **See page 102.**

The Circus Tavern's bar counter is shoe-horned beneath the stairs. Footballing legend George Best used to stand drinking beside it.

Below stairs bar counter – with room for just one server
The Circus Tavern, 86 Portland Street, M1 4GX. Tel: 07863 349957.

It's just as well that this diminutive pub offers table service as any more than a score of customers makes it packed. On my visit the barmaid claimed the official limit was 70 people: 'Sometimes it's difficult to count them though. We've had two rugby teams in here at once and that was a lively occasion,' she said. The three-storey frontage in the city centre is so narrow it's easy to miss. Entering, you are just a couple of paces from an arc-shaped bar counter, shoe-horned beneath the stairs beside the hallway. It is so small only one staff member can serve there. In front is the corner where iconic winger George Best would stand to drink (there are photos of him on the wall) and behind is a door and steps leading, precipitously, to the cellar. There are two public rooms off a narrow corridor, each with decorative fireplaces and bench seating. Photographs of the city's two famous football teams cover the walls. Two cask ales were being served, Tetley Bitter and Robinson's Dizzy Blonde. It is named after a nearby Circus Hall demolished in 1805 and is deservedly popular with tourists and football fans alike. On CAMRA's National Inventory; no food.

By boot: **See page 102.**

Tiled extravaganza outside, Victorian gem inside
Peveril of the Peak, 127 Great Bridgewater Street, M1 5JQ. Tel. 0161 236 6364.

Shiny ceramic tiling covering almost the entire exterior gives this pub the look of one of those glazed cottage models sold in souvenir shops. Installed around 1900, the porcelain decoration includes ornate door and window surrounds with floral motifs above. Spurning a conventional inn sign, the pub's name is highlighted in large ceramic lettering on both sides – its strange shape occupies a corner site. The interior is equally pleasing – full of polished woodwork and stained glass – notably in an oddly-shaped drinking lobby with a decorative glazed screen around the servery windows. There are three rooms, including a public bar and smoke room with its marble fire surround, fitted bench seating, potted palms and bell-pushes, once used to summon waitresses. Photos show celebrity customers including the Gallagher brothers from Oasis, actor-comedian Robbie Coltrane and author Bill Bryson. There are four hand-pumps, offering ales from Copper Dragon, Seven Brothers, Timothy Taylor and Adnams when I visited. A classic Bob Dylan album was playing, which made up in atmosphere for a dearth of customers. The pub takes its name from that of a 'light post coach', carrying eight passengers, that linked Manchester and London daily, taking a bone-shaking twenty-three hours in the pre-railway age. On CAMRA's National Inventory; no food.

By boot: **See page 102.**

Century-old ceramic tiling covers every inch of the Peveril of the Peak's exterior.

Subterranean public toilet
The Temple, 100 Great Bridgewater Street, M1 5JW. Tel. 0161 278 1610.

Its full title is Temple of Convenience, for reasons that will be immediately apparent when you arrive. The entrance is behind railings in the middle of the road and you descend a series of steps to reach your destination. This former public convenience has been minimally adapted into a subterranean drinking den. It's attractive in a Bohemian sort of way – but not the ideal venue for a first date, as one customer put it. There's no real ale but a good selection of bottled world beers, while Tetley's and Guinness were on draught. A juke-box has a fine selection of music, including Mancunian bands and classic rock, with the Beatles' White Album playing while I was there. Dimly-lit and

Watering hole: entrance to the Temple, a pub in a public convenience.

decorated with event posters and brewery signs. When I visited the toilet, I was intrigued to find original white ceramic walls overlaid with topical urban street art and graffiti. Cool. No food.

By boot: See below.

Manchester on foot

The city is easy to navigate on foot and all four pubs featured here are central and within an easy walk of each other. For longer city journeys, and jaunts to pub-rich places such as Eccles and Bury, the Metrolink service is frequent and easy to use. For those seeking a longer challenge, the 39-mile Bridgewater Way is perfect, following the historic Bridgewater Canal through Cheshire, Greater Manchester and Lancashire. The route is being developed and goes via Salford, Trafford, Warrington and Runcorn, towards the Mersey estuary. When complete it will be suitable for cyclists too. Details at www.bridgewatercanal.co.uk

MARGATE, KENT

Fishermen's sheds on a jetty

The Lighthouse Bar / Harbour Arms, CT9 1JD.
Lighthouse: Tel. 01843 291153. www.lighthousebar.co.uk.
Harbour Arms: Tel. 07776 183273.
www.the-harbour-arms.co.uk

These two hostelries, which are separate businesses, occupy adapted fishermen's stores within a few hundred yards of each other on the Harbour Arm, a jetty just a few minutes' walk from the Turner Contemporary Gallery. The Lighthouse Bar is a compact hideaway beneath a 66ft-tall marine light built in the 1950s. Customers enjoy superb harbour and sea views from

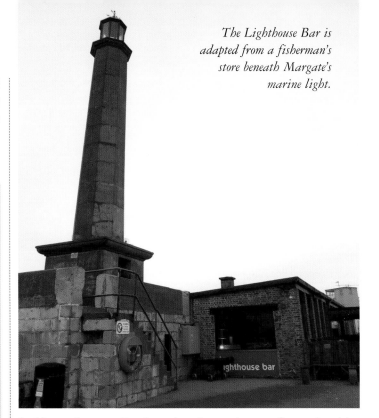

The Lighthouse Bar is adapted from a fisherman's store beneath Margate's marine light.

inside and out. Outdoor bench seating, sofas and tables overlook the beach and promenade: perfect on a calm day. Indoors, you can contemplate the bay in all weathers through picture windows. I claimed one of the sofas at the seaward end to enjoy an uninterrupted panorama of sand, sea and sky of the sort that brought the artist J.M.W. Turner to Margate. A long, thin bar, with bare brick walls and floorboards, is minimally decorated with modern art and a log burner on a pebbled hearth. I found no real ale but Krombacher beer was on keg and there are bottled beers. Food served; dogs welcome; ambient music plus regular live sessions.

The Harbour Arms is a micropub, with fishermen's nets, other maritime items and ale casks scattered about. A haven for real ale fans, four tasty micro brews were available on my visit, from Burton Bridge, Raw, Brew Buddies and Red Star. There were also at least four scrumpy ciders, basic bar snacks and a sign advertising Margate Harbour mud packs for sale (I think the latter was a joke). Despite its limited space there is an assortment of seating, including high stools, farmhouse chairs and high backed settles. There is outdoor seating facing the beach but no electronic entertainment and no toilets. Public conveniences are situated a few yards along the jetty. Dog friendly. While in town, don't miss another micropub, the Lifeboat in Market Street, which has a stone floor, fireplace, benches inside and out and beer casks forming a central focal point.

By boot and bike: Close to the Viking Coastal trail (NCN Regional Route 15), a 32-mile circular trail around the Isle of Thanet, including Broadstairs (see page 33) and Ramsgate. *By boat:* If you have your own sea-going vessel, you can moor outside.

This hat stand is one of many odd exhibits in the canal-side Folly Inn, Napton.

NAPTON ON THE HILL, WARWICKSHIRE

Canal-side pub that thinks it's a museum
The Folly Inn, Folly Lane, CV47 8NZ.
Tel. 01926 815185. http://thefollyinn.co.uk/

A hat-stand sets the theme to this rather eccentric place. It is loaded with British and German military helmets, a bowler hat, an African pith helmet, a leopard skin millinery piece Boy George would be proud of and two ambulance-men's helmets, with visors. A Turkish fez and another bowler hang, inexplicably, from a pair of antlers, which in turn are sited near a strategically placed gramophone horn and hunting bugle. This canal-side pub is a welcome sight for thirsty narrow-boaters who have negotiated the flight of nine locks which form a formidable obstacle for sailors on the Oxford Canal. Napton Windmill is a useful landmark for those searching out the pub, which is hidden at the end of a narrow lane near a boaters' shop.

Starting life as a farmhouse, it became the Bull and Butcher pub, a popular stopping point for working boatmen when the canal carried much of the freight between the Midlands and London. After a long period of closure when the canal fell into disuse from the 1940s, it reopened in 1992. Now a cosy, oak-beamed hostelry with two bars, one with a large inglenook fireplace, the other with an equally warming wood-burning stove, the Folly is the nearest thing you will find to a museum with bar attached. There is no obvious theme to the exhibits. In addition to hats, there are collections of bottles, plates, teapots, clocks, cameras and figurines. Paintings, photos and enigmatic portraits fill every available space on the walls; leather saddles await their horses and hurricane and miners' lamps hang from beams. Hundreds of objects line the windowsills, mantelpieces and yards of high shelves. Whoever has the job of dusting it all must be patient and dextrous. I was told the objects were collected by the landlord, Mark, whose collection just seemed to grow and grow. The rustic furniture includes candle-lit tables, but this is a drinker's as well as a diner's bolt-hole (that said it is advisable to book if you are dining in summer). Real ales included, on my visit, examples from Hook Norton, and guests Phipps NBC Steamroller and North Cotswold Shagweaver, as well as real ciders and perry. The menu includes steaks and homemade pies, vegetarian and fish dishes. Dog friendly (and human tolerant, according to the website); large garden.

By bike: East of NCN Route 48 (Lincoln-Exeter) at Southam. *By boat:* Moor beside bridge 113 on the Oxford Canal.

NEWCASTLE UPON TYNE, TYNE AND WEAR

Music from a vintage gramophone
Crown Posada, 31 The Side, NE1 3JE.
Tel. 0191 232 1269. www.sjf.co.uk

Two minutes' walk from Grey Street, this Newcastle institution is one of the city's oldest pubs. It is atmospheric, ornate and fount of a regularly changing variety of real ales (six on my visit). The background music is generated, at a sensible volume, on a piece of equipment that is at least sixty years old. Sitting on the bar counter, next to a case of vinyl LPs and a tray full of pork scratchings, is a Dynatron Cavalcade record player.

In the groove: the sixty-year-old Dynatron Cavalcade gramophone that provides music in the Crown Posada.

This sees almost constant use, playing a variety of timeless hits. The barman told me the set, in its varnished wooden cabinet, dates from 1941 but since the Dynatron was a popular model manufactured for many years, I cannot substantiate this fact. It is, however, treated with affection and has a unique sound. It also requires the constant ear of bar staff, since as older readers will know, an LP needs to be changed or turned over every twenty minutes or so. Though long and narrow in size and shape, the pub has a place on CAMRA's National Inventory, as it retains three distinctive drinking areas. The cosiest of these is a small, wood-screened snug with glass panels, upholstered bench seating and a vintage GEC wireless. There are also delightfully detailed Pre-Raphaelite style stained glass windows, a decorative ceiling and wall paintings which are behind wallpaper so only seen when the place is redecorated. The pub was rebuilt in 1880 for Newcastle brewer John Sanderson and is Grade II listed. No meals served but sandwiches are often available.

By boot and bike: Situated just off the Quayside Hadrian's Way (cycle route 72).

Its well-worn look is part of local folklore
Free Trade Inn, St Lawrence Road, Byker, NE6 1AP.
Tel. 0191 265 5764

Don't be fooled by the yellowing paint flaking off the walls, the linoleum floors or the graffiti-strewn loos: they are part of the pub's scruffy image. It was among a select band of 50 eccentric hostelries that made it into the *Rough Pub Guide* (Orion Books, London, 2008, page 120). The book claims Jimi Hendrix enjoyed the hostelry while staying nearby with ex-Animal Chas Chandler, but these days the clientele is as likely to be students and builders as artists and musicians. Everyone seems to love this place, though that may be something to do with the choice of eight real ales, cider and Belgian and other foreign beers served, and the free juke-box loaded with several decades' worth of classic hits. There is 'the best view in Newcastle' of the River

A Tyneside sunset reflected in the windows of the Free Trade Inn, Byker.

Tyne and its bridges far below, seen either through picture windows or from one of the two beer gardens. I enjoyed a golden autumnal sunset while supping a Durham Magus (ABV 3.8%) sitting next to two bicycles that were parked in the bar. Snacks range from pies and sandwiches to samosas, Scotch eggs and somewhat incongruously, 'gluten free cakes'. CAMRA Tyneside Cider pub of the year 2015.

By boot and bike: Situated above the Hadrian's Way path along the river (cycle route 72). Bike hire and spares available from the Byker Cycle Hub on the quayside adjacent.

Tudor house with a 'wall of windows'— and a micro-brewery

Hop and Cleaver, 40 Sandhill, NE1 3RG.
Tel. 0191 261 1037. www.hopandcleaver.com

Part of a group of Jacobean style merchants' houses and shops and a remarkable sight on the city's quayside. Built to impress in an era when window tax made glazing expensive, as was

Bessie Surtees' house next-door, which is in the care of Historic England and open to visitors. Bessie was the building's most famous resident, who descended a ladder in 1772 to elope with a young gentleman who later became Britain's Lord Chancellor. The Hop and Cleaver is an American-style smokehouse, opened in 2014 complete with a micro-brewery purchased from Temptation Brewery at Houghton-le-Spring, on full view to customers. Home brews, including Black Beard Stout, Quayside Pale and Pearl Harbour, are served in third-pint tasting trays: there is also a wide choice of guest ales and speciality bourbons. The interior has been stripped back to bare brick and stone walls and floors, with heavy timbers and cast-iron pillars supporting the ceilings. Imported wood-fired ovens are used to create the steaks and smokehouse specialities of the house. The labyrinthine building deserves exploration, as it not only reveals the aforementioned micro-brewery but leads to an adjoining pub. With its tiled floor and brick-built oven, the Red House (tel. 0191 261 1037) has a more intimate feel than its neighbour. The ale selection is slightly different and the food menu has a pie-and-mash theme. There are also cobbled and tiled passageways, disused doorways, a cosy snug bar, a tunnel

Two pubs, the Hop and Cleaver and the Red House, occupy this Jacobean merchant's house on Newcastle's quayside.

vault with seating and other period features.

By boot and bike: Situated just off the Quayside Hadrian's Way (cycle route 72). *By boat:* Close to the quayside, from where regular Tyne sightseeing cruises operate from March to October.

NORTON ST PHILIP, SOMERSET

Unchanged in 300 years – and a film star
The George Inn, High Street, BA2 7LH.
Tel. 01373 834224. www.georgeinnnsp.co.uk

Ale has been served for more than 600 years at this half-timbered medieval inn. Ever since Carthusian monks built a resting place for merchants and travellers in the late fourteenth century, when the town's cloth fairs were in full swing. Largely unchanged for the last 300 years, it was superbly restored by Wadworth Brewery in the 1990s. To step into the cobbled courtyard and the bars is to journey back through time. Diarist Samuel Pepys 'dined well' there for ten shillings and the Duke

of Monmouth used it as his headquarters shortly before his defeat at the Battle of Sedgemoor in 1685. Legend has it that there was an attempt on his life: a shot was fired as he was shaving by a window. Though the assassination attempt failed, Monmouth, the illegitimate son of Charles II, was later beheaded on Tower Hill for leading the rebellion. Twelve of his compatriots were hanged outside the inn after being condemned by the infamous Judge Jeffreys. These days the only shooting that goes on is for films and television. The George was used as a setting for *The Remains of the Day*, *Tom Jones* (when Albert Finney leapt from the gallery) and *The Canterbury Tales*, while producers of the television versions of *Moll Flanders* and *Persuasion* also found it suitably photogenic.

There is a succession of spacious rooms, timbered galleries, a medieval stair-tower and magnificent oak-trussed roof. At the time of my visit two rooms were in use as bars, the most impressive being the Board Room with its large stone fireplace, wood floor, oak-beamed ceiling and fifteenth-century bay window. This is furnished with benches, settles and tables and was atmospherically candle-lit on a bright afternoon. A wood-case clock and historical prints decorated the walls. There were

Medieval cloth fairs were held in and around the George Inn, Norton St Philip. Actor Albert Finney leapt from its gallery more recently.

This 1913 postcard of the George Inn explains its notoriety as site of a failed assassination attempt on the Duke of Monmouth.

three ales on sale, all from the Wadworth's stable, namely 6X, Henry's IPA and Swordfish. Across the cobbled passage is the Monmouth, or Dungeon Bar, which was formerly the cellar and is much darker, with a rough-hewn stone floor and walls. There is a walled garden laid with grass, planted with lavender and offering a stunning view across the valley to the hills beyond. Toilets are across the courtyard. A wide ranging menu includes puddings and a selection of local cheeses. Grade 1 listed; accommodation available.

By boot: The village is 7 miles from Bath and well served by footpaths. For example, you could walk to Tucker's Grave Inn at Faulkland (page 60). *By bike:* Two miles south of NCN Route 24 which goes from Bath through Radstock, Frome and Warminster.

NORWICH, NORFOLK

Gallery of inn signs – and a 'free mouse'
The Fat Cat, 49 West End Street, NR2 4NA.
Tel. 01603 624364. http://fatcatpub.co.uk

There's the Green Man, the Half Moon, the Royal William and the Local Hero (Admiral Lord Nelson, in case you wondered). The inn signs that adorn the walls are works of art; as are the veteran brewery signs from old local companies – Lacons, Bullards, Steward and Patteson among them. The collection of pub memorabilia and breweriana is a good reason to visit but beer, cider and perry aficionados will tell you the Cat is, as it says outside, a 'free mouse' best known for its incredible drink selection. It has twice been CAMRA National Pub of the Year and has won other awards too numerous to list. The line-up of hand-pumps and casks offered me a choice of 30-plus ales, including some from their eponymous brewery, plus a range of Belgian delicacies among other bottled beers. Sympathetically converted from a run-down, back street boozer in 1991, this brick-built corner hostelry has a variety of seating areas, a black-and-white tiled floor and partitions decorated with

The Fat Cat, Norwich doubles as a gallery of veteran inn and brewery signs, and enamel advertisements. It has a great reputation for ale and cider, too.

stained glass. It is invariably busy with customers, many of whom have made long pilgrimages to get here. Now that's what you call a good sign. Snack foods; outside seating; dog friendly.

By boot: About thirty minutes from Norwich Station but well worth the walk. *By bike:* Less than a mile east of East Coast (Dover-Shetland Islands) NCN Route 1.

NOTTINGHAM, NOTTINGHAMSHIRE

Canal flows inside – with boats moored near the bar
The Canal House, 48-52 Canal Street, NG1 7EH. Tel: 0115 9555060. www.thecanalhouse.co.uk

A former warehouse for Fellows Morton and Clayton – once the biggest canal transport company – then a canal museum, this four-storey brick leviathan is where the Industrial Revolution meets twenty-first century hedonism. Opened as a pub in 2000, the interior is cavernous and relatively little changed. There are

Narrow-boats at rest in the Canal House, Nottingham. The footbridge links a seating area with the main bar, the counter of which runs almost the entire length of the building.

solid wooden floors, massive iron beams and a long, rivet-studded bar counter fitted with banks of hand-pumps and craft beer taps. Where narrow-boats once sailed in to be unloaded, two boats are moored, a few feet from the bar (reached via a footbridge). Outside, beside a wharf, is a sun-trap cobbled courtyard, with bench seating, overlooked by two old iron cranes. A large function room upstairs can hold 200 people. Real ales from Castle Rock, Fuller's and Batemans were available, plus 150 bottled world beers and 13 real ciders. Food served; ambient music.

By boot and bike: **Near the railway station. The Nottingham & Beeston Canal towpath passes and links with the River Trent, providing a 10-mile walk or cycle ride from Trent Bridge to Beeston Lock, via the city** centre, known as the Big Track. Links to NCN Route 6. *By boat:* **Visitor mooring at Castle Marina on the canal (near city centre, postcode NG7 1TN) with access to the tidal and non-tidal Trent.**

Pub in cave

Hand and Heart, 65 Derby Road, Nottingham NG1 5BA. Tel. 0115 958 2456. www.thehandandheart.co.uk

This is a city with its own 'underworld'. It is built on soft rock which proved easy to excavate. Cliffs and outcrops have been hollowed out since medieval times to provide useful warehouses and the ancient equivalent of industrial units – more than 400 of them. There are several pubs utilising caverns, one of the most extensive being the ancient Trip to Jerusalem (q.v.). The Hand and Heart is almost 200 years old and, apart from the section facing the street, which includes an *upstairs* conservatory, is situated mainly in a cave. The premises became a brewery in the 1860s, with the caves used for beer storage. It reopened in 2008, following a four-year closure and restoration from a state of near dereliction. The focal point is a large sandstone cavern that has become an atmospheric, candle-lit dining area. There are cosy drinking nooks, too and a visit to the gents' toilet felt like entering Fred Flintstone's house in prehistoric Bedrock. There is a chandelier in a sandstone 'chimney'. Five real ales on my visit included examples from Dancing Duck and Maypole and real cider. Meals served; regular live music; dog friendly.

By boot and bike: See Canal House, page 108. The pub is about a mile north-west of the canal towpath and railway station.

A man-made cavern, formerly used for beer storage, is now a candle-lit dining area of the Hand and Heart, Nottingham. Even the gents' toilet occupies a cave.

ODCOMBE, SOMERSET

Thatched smokers' retreat

Mason's Arms, 41 Lower Odcombe, near Yeovil, BA22 8TX. Tel. 01935 862591. www.masonsarmsodcombe.co.uk

Thatched smokers' hut in the floral garden of the Mason's Arms, Odcombe.

Cycling along narrow, sunken lanes on a hot summer's afternoon to find this stone-built, thatched inn in a bucolic village, was a joy. It serves ale from its own micro-brewery, reopened in 2005, with three home brews regularly available, including the flagship Odcombe No.1. Dining is popular (booking advised). One table is set into an inglenook fireplace. The pub boasts the only *thatched* smokers' retreat I have ever seen. At many pubs, smokers must contend with an ugly lean-to or shed-like structure. Here, they have their own rural idyll, lovingly crafted from wood, with integral bench seating, placed in a cottage-style garden filled with lavender and hollyhock. I half expected a nineteenth-century character, wearing a smock and clutching a clay pipe, to emerge from the den's spacious confines. Accommodation available; campsite adjacent; dog friendly.

By bike: On the 128-mile South Somerset Cycle Route (Ilminster-Yeovil).

OXFORD, OXFORDSHIRE

The ultimate tie collection

The Bear, 6 Alfred Street, OX1 4EH. Tel. 01865 728164.
www.bearoxford.co.uk

A wood-panelled rear room, including the ceiling, is covered with 24 glass cases full of men's ties. Four thousand of them, unceremoniously snipped off with scissors. More cases are in the front bar, though that bar's low, wood-beamed ceiling presumably ruled itself out for the grabatologist (tie collector) who started this unorthodox collection in 1952. According to the *Encyclopaedia of Oxford* (Macmillan, 1988) that was landlord Alan Course, a newspaper cartoonist. In return for having their ties shortened, donors were given a free drink, a tradition that has long since stopped due to lack of space. The hostelry features in Colin Dexter's Inspector Morse novel *Death is Now My Neighbour*, where the detective seeks the landlord's peculiar expertise. The neckwear displayed is carefully captioned, including examples from rowing, golf, sailing and rugby clubs;

The author surrounded by some of the thousands of ties in the Bear, Oxford.

army battalions and veterans' societies; veritable 'old school ties' from Eton and Harrow and others from the world's universities and military academies. I spotted one belonging to an ex-prisoner of war in the Wooden Horse Club (presumably an escapee from Stalag Luft III); another from a hero of the Somme in WWI, marked 'Personal tie of Capt. Paul Bennett, VC, MC, 2nd Batt. Worcestershire Regiment.'

The whitewashed pub is small, wood floored and cosy, especially on a winter's evening when a fire blazes and conversation fills the bar. It dates from the early seventeenth century – though there was an inn here centuries before – and on that basis claims to be the city's oldest. A century later, it was the departure point for the 'Oxford Machine', a stage-coach to London. Among the celebrities that have visited are actors Richard Burton and Elizabeth Taylor and former US President Bill Clinton. Tourists from many nations flock here. The bar stocks a wide range of London brewer Fuller's real ales, as well as the local Shotover Oxford Scholar (ABV 4.5%). Meals served; live music weekly; open-air terrace; bike parking at rear.

By boot: **The city has a wide variety of pubs, many of them within walking distance. Several companies, such as Footprints Tours, offer guided walks on a pub theme. *By bike:* Central Oxford has a high level of cycling and is on NCN Route 5 (Reading-Holyhead); the Thames Valley Route (NCN 4/5) continues to London via Windsor.**

PETERBOROUGH, CAMBRIDGESHIRE

A Dutch barge

Charters, Town Bridge, PE1 1FP. Tel. 01733 315700.
www.charters-bar.com

The riverside gardens, lit with garlands of lights, are filled with drinkers and diners at a barbeque. Other customers cross a gangplank to fetch their pints from below deck. Swans glide on the water. It's a warm summer evening beside the *Leendert-R*, a 176ft-long Dutch grain barge, built in 1907. This isn't a scene

A summer's night on the River Nene at Peterborough, showing the Leendert-R, *a Dutch grain barge that is home to Charters pub and restaurant. Ale is served from 12 handpumps below deck.*

from Amsterdam or the Hook of Holland but the River Nene in the middle of Peterborough. When the vessel retired from grain-carrying duties it was brought across the North Sea, moored beside Town Bridge and converted to a floating pub-restaurant, opening in 1991. I was told that the boat had to be 'sunk' and refloated in order to get it under the bridge but that may be a tall tale from an old sea-dog. In 2016 it celebrated its twenty-fifth anniversary as a pub. The bar in the hold, with its wooden floor and bench seating, has a lengthy counter, lined with 12 hand-pumps. These were dispensing four ales from Oakham Brewery and guests from Milestone, Saffron and Magpie on my visit, plus several real ciders. Details are chalked on a blackboard. With rivets and ropes on display and hard wearing furniture – no plush sofas here – there's a real maritime feel. The top deck offers a complete contrast – a cosy Pan Asian restaurant, East, its tables set with white tablecloths. Regular live music in bar; riverside beer garden with seasonal bar; dog friendly.

By boot: The 114-mile Nene Way follows the river from Badby, Northamptonshire to Sutton Bridge, Lincolnshire.

A much shorter footpath from the garden leads to the Nene Valley heritage railway. *By bike:* Just off NCN Routes 63 (Burton-Wisbech), 53 (Peterborough-Birmingham) and 12 (Enfield-Spalding). *By boat:* The River Nene is 100 miles long, has 38 locks and is popular with narrow-boaters. Charters has its own landing stage.

PIEL ISLAND, CUMBRIA

Landlord is 'King of Piel' – pub reached by ferry

The Ship Inn, via Roa Island, LA13 0QN.
Tel. 07516 453784. www.pielisland.co.uk

You can walk around Piel Island (population: four) in fifteen minutes. Its twin focal points are the ruins of a castle that was once second in size to the Tower of London – and this whitewashed pub. The Ship is notable for its isolation, its wonderful views and, maintaining a tradition going back hundreds of years, its landlord holds the title King of Piel. Of the three slate-floored public rooms, the bar is cosiest, with curved settle seating and a solid fuel stove set in a large stone fireplace. An aged oak chair rests beside it. This is the 'throne' used for the king's coronation and knighting ceremonies, which involve pouring a jug of ale over the subject's head. The current monarch, landlord Steve Chattaway, was crowned in September 2008 and the ancient regalia, including a helmet and sword, is displayed in a secure cabinet. The tradition of having a king is said to pay mocking homage to a 1487 uprising against the English throne, led by merchant's son Lambert Simnel who began an ill-fated invasion by landing on Piel with German and Irish mercenaries. He was defeated by Henry VII's army just twelve days later. Those honoured to become Knights of Piel (a tradition dating from 1856) are expected to buy everyone a drink and – be warned – anyone sitting on the throne by mistake must do the same. By decree, the king and his knights are required to be 'a drinker, smoker and ardent lover of the opposite sex.' Its garden has one of the finest views from any

The Piel Island ferry returning with a boat-load of customers from the Ship Inn, the whitewashed building in the distance. Piel Castle can also been seen.

pub: a panorama of Morecambe Bay, with boats to-ing and fro-ing and, in the distance, the Cumbrian fells. This vista was accompanied on my summer visit by bird-song. The inn is a listed building and was restored in 2010, which included the installation of a 'cabinet of curiosities.' This covers a whole wall and includes local memorabilia, ranging from 'cave coral' and 'pearls of sea mussels' to photos and models of warships and airships built in neighbouring Barrow-in-Furness. Two ales specially brewed by Ulverston Brewery – Piel Princess (ABV 4%) and King Stephen (4.2%) – were on hand-pump. Jars of sweets were items rarely seen on a bar counter. Meals served; B&B accommodation and camping (obtain permit from landlord); dog friendly. Closed Mondays in low season. There is no road access. A pedestrian ferry makes the short crossing to Piel from Roa Island: operation is seasonal, from Easter and subject to weather conditions. Check with pub if in doubt.

By boot: An enjoyable way of reaching Piel Island is by following part of the 182-mile Cumbria Coastal Way/Cistercian Way from Roose near Barrow-in-Furness (there are railway stations at both). It follows the estuarine sands, linking with a causeway to Roa Island, from where you take the ferry. The distance is about 3 miles. OS Explorer Map OL6.

PONTFAEN, PEMBROKESHIRE

In the family since 1845 – beer is served from a jug
Dyffryn Arms, SA65 9SE. Tel. 01348 881305.

This pebble-dashed house, built in 1845 in a tranquil valley in the Pembrokeshire Coast National Park, is among the last survivors of the once everyday simple country pub. It has hardly changed in a hundred years. There's no inn sign, no bar counter in the single bar room, no hand-pumps, no music and only the most basic furniture and decoration. Yet it has been visited by HRH The Prince of Wales and is on CAMRA's National

The Dyffryn Arms, a traditional beer-house in the beautiful Gwaun Valley. It is looked after by eighty-five-year-old Bessie Davies.

Inventory of pub interiors. It is also known as 'Bessie's', after eighty-five-year-old landlady Bessie Davies, who has run the place for forty-five years. Instead of a bar there's a sliding hatch in the wall and you ring a bell for attention. There's no food and the choice of drink is limited: customers choose between the local Gwynt y Ddraig cider and Bass ale, which is decanted into a jug from casks behind the counter. You've guessed, there is no beer cellar either. This is one of only two pubs in Wales to serve beer in this way (see also the Cresselly Arms, page 48). It was a pleasure to meet the quietly spoken Bessie, holding court in an armchair in the quarry-tiled bar. With its high-backed box settle, benches, stone fireplace and portrait of the Queen hanging from a picture rail, it doubles as her front-room. Banknotes from dozens of countries are displayed, indicating the international popularity of the hostelry. The pub keeps the ancient tradition of Hen Galan, where the New Year is welcomed in on January 13th, according to the old Gregorian calendar. Conversation in Welsh is often heard. A grassy garden provides views of the wooded valley. Dog friendly.

By boot: The Cwm Gwaun valley is perfect walking country. *By bike:* On the Celtic Trail West, NCN Route 47 (Fishguard-Swansea).

PORTISHEAD, SOMERSET

Built from shipping containers

Hall & Woodhouse Bar & Restaurant, Portishead Quays Marina, 59 Newfoundland Way, BS20 7FP. Tel. 01275 848685. www.hall-woodhouseportishead.co.uk

Once a busy docks, Portishead has been gentrified and transformed into a marina with several trendy eating and drinking establishments. None are as quirky as this one: a bright, contemporary development by Dorset brewers Hall & Woodhouse. It opened in 2013 and won CAMRA's Design Award the following year, in the Best New Pub category. In the words of the judges, 'It looks entirely at home on the quayside.'

Freight-diner: The Hall & Woodhouse Bar is built from shipping containers. It overlooks Portishead Marina and has won CAMRA's Design Award for Best New Pub.

They could have added that it offers good views too, especially from the upstairs restaurant. They continue: 'The bar and shelving are made out of plain unvarnished wood, adding to the maritime feel of the structure.' The interior decor also features industrial lamps, huge girders and, upstairs, some of the containers have been transformed into snugs. Even the toilets have porthole windows. There were three of the company's Badger Beers on hand-pump, and a wide food menu. Breakfast available; bench seating outside; ambient music.

By boot: The marina is an ideal location for a short waterside walk. *By bike:* Portishead is 11 miles from Bristol using the delightful River Avon path, via the Avon Gorge and Pill, much of it traffic free. NCN Routes 33 and 41. *By boat:* Portishead Quays is a well-equipped marina with short and long stay berthing.

PORTLAND, DORSET

On an 18-mile beach – survivor of storms and floods

Cove House Inn, 91 Chiswell, DT5 1AW.
Tel. 01305 820895. http://thecovehouseinn.co.uk

The location is idyllic on a fine day and hypnotic on a stormy one. This centuries-old pub stands, isolated, yards from Chesil Beach, which stretches unbroken for 18 miles. Sunsets over Lyme Bay are spectacular, with great views from seats inside and benches outside. Built, like a fortress, out of large stone blocks and protected by a concrete flood wall with reinforced iron gates, the pub is ready to cope with the worst Mother Nature can – and does – throw at it. Inside, bare wood floors, stone walls, low ceilings and a real fire reveal a place little changed since Victorian fishermen sought shelter and refreshment. Photographs line the walls, illustrating a history of storms, shipwrecks, floods and the pub's survival against the odds. One shows the building cloaked in pounding waves, foam and drifting spray, taking on a hurricane force gale. Another reveals Chiswell village under several feet of water. One wall is set out as a gallery showing some of the many ships that have been wrecked over hundreds of years, with considerable loss of life. In a BBC interview about storms, landlady Amanda Broughton-

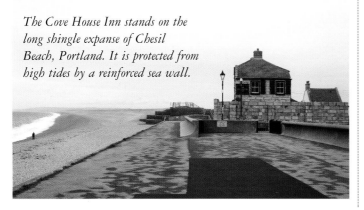

The Cove House Inn stands on the long shingle expanse of Chesil Beach, Portland. It is protected from high tides by a reinforced sea wall.

South said '... [our] bedrooms have been flooded, windows have been smashed by pebbles, roof slates have gone and outside lights have been ripped off walls.' The weather was benign on my visit, when three ales were available: Wells' Bombardier, Adnams Broadside and Sharp's Doom Bar. The menu has a maritime flavour, including crab and fisherman's pie. Dog friendly; folk music weekly.

By boot: Situated on the 13-mile Isle of Portland circuit of the South West Coast Path National Trail. Walking the beach itself is tough, however, being almost all shingle, and part is not accessible in summer to protect nesting birds. *By bike:* When complete, NCN Route 26 will run from Portland Bill to Portishead on the Somerset coast.

RIPLEY, SURREY

Magnet for Victorian cyclists

The Anchor, High Street, GU23 6AE. Tel. 01483 211866.
www.ripleyanchor.co.uk

For three decades from 1870, a 30-mile stretch of the London to Portsmouth turnpike road was a race-track for thousands of riders on their new-fangled Penny Farthings and other velocipedes. In particular, the 10 miles between two watering holes, the Angel Inn at Thames Ditton and this timber-framed hotel became famous as the 'Ripley Road'. These days, the Anchor, which was bought by local restaurateurs in 2013, is better known as a gastro-pub serving dishes such as pheasant and ham terrine than as a 'liquid lunch' stop for cyclists. Its contemporary interior is dotted with appropriate decorations – a vintage cycling board game here, metal bicycle miniatures there. Of several oak-beamed rooms, the oldest is a central bar that dates from its beginning as an almshouse in the sixteenth century. When Ripley, thanks to its copious inns, earned its reputation as 'the Mecca of all good cyclists,' (Lord Bury, 1887) the Anchor was favourite. This was thanks to its efficient landlady, Mrs Dibble and her pretty daughters Annie and Harriet. So popular were they that, on the daughters' deaths in the 1890s, cyclists subscribed towards a memorial window in the adjacent parish church, St Mary's. Another to be seen is dedicated to Herbert Liddell Cortis, the first man to ride a Penny Farthing 20 miles in an hour (1882). It is likely that he boasted about his exploits over a pint next door, too. The historical Anchor's cyclists' visitor books, signed by up to 6000 riders annually from 1881-95, are kept at Surrey History Centre in Woking.

Above: *Penny Farthings and velocipedes pose outside the Anchor at Ripley,* circa *1896, when it was 'the Mecca of all good cyclists.'*
Below: *Members of the Veteran-Cycle Club pose outside the Anchor with their vintage machines in 2016, at the start of their sixtieth anniversary ride to London.*

At weekends a steady stream of cyclists pedal through the village and, occasionally, vintage bike owners pause at the inn for old time's sake. In May 2016, the author photographed members of the Veteran-Cycle Club at the start of its sixtieth anniversary run from Ripley to Hyde Park. The owners of Penny Farthings and Sunbeams posed with those of Dursley Pedersens and a Boneshaker, echoing photos taken with plate cameras a hundred years before. Two ales were served on my visit, Timothy Taylor Landlord and Courage Best. Ambient music; sheltered outside dining area.

By boot: Ripley is one of seven stages on the 39-mile Fox Way, a circuit of walks in the Guildford area.

ROSEBUSH, PEMBROKESHIRE

Built of galvanized iron – has a railway station in the garden

Tafarn Sinc, Maenclochog, Clunderwen, SA66 7QU.
Tel. 01437 532214. www.tafarnsinc.co.uk

More akin to a mountain lodge than a pub, this red-painted hideaway was built in 1876 as a railway hotel, using corrugated galvanized iron. The line, from Clunderwen, closed to passengers in 1937 but the hotel and its pleasure gardens survived until 1992, by which time they were in a bad state of repair. It was bought by two locals, refurbished and reopened as a pub. With sweeping views to the Preseli Mountains, it claims to be the highest licensed premises in the county. Wooden, sawdust-covered floors, wood-panelled walls and tongue-and-groove ceilings – hung with tools, lamps, dried hams and sheaves of wheat – combine to create a rustic look. The furniture, including settles, has a lived-in appearance, while wood-burner stoves provide warmth on cooler days. There is a long main bar with snugs and a large dining room with picture windows. The remnants of Rosebush Station platforms can be discerned in the garden, which has bench seating. The landlords have let their imagination run free in an artistic recreation of

Remnants of Rosebush railway station – including dummy 'passengers' – decorate the beer garden of Tafarn Sinc in the foothills of the Preseli Mountains. The station closed in 1937.

the halt, complete with waiting shelter, signs, milk churn and dummy passengers awaiting a train that will never come. It was busy on a September lunchtime and my friend Graham and I arrived in time for last food orders at 2pm. Three real ales were available, namely the locally brewed Cwrw Tafarn Sinc (ABV 3.6%), W.H. Buckley Best and Worthington's Cask. There is a dartboard, assorted memorabilia and historic photos on show and you are likely to hear Welsh being spoken. Closed Monday out of season; ambient music. The Gwaun Valley Brewery welcomes visitors at nearby Pontfaen.

By boot: A section of the Pembrokeshire Trail begins in Rosebush and ends in the riverside hamlet of Gelli.

ROYSTON, HERTFORDSHIRE

Former post office – sit in a Royal Mail van

The Jolly Postie, 2 Baldock Street, SG8 5AY.
Tel. 01763 248734. www.mcmullens.co.uk/jollypostie

If you enjoyed playing post offices as a child, this is where you can sample the grown-up version, with alcohol and comfort food replacing toy money and stamps. The distinctive building was the town's main P.O. from 1935, more recently becoming a pub called the Barracuda, then the Old Crown, which closed in 2013. Hertfordshire brewer McMullen & Sons took over, commissioning a makeover celebrating the philatelic past in an amusing and stylish way. It opened as the Jolly Postie in 2015. The exterior retains its stamp machines, though sadly non-operational, plus there's a three-dimensional inn sign consisting of a postman riding a real bicycle, letters flying in his wake. The next eye-catching feature is a veteran Austin Morris LD Royal Mail van parked inside, beside the entrance. In the vehicle's rear, where sacks were stacked, there is a table and seating for eight. Other genuine features dotted around include a red telephone box, a pillar box, hand trolleys (some set into tables) and a plethora of red delivery bicycles. These are also seen in profusion in the patio garden, including one forming part of a gate. Observe mail sacks used as cushions, a real fire in a 'bonded goods' store, a postman 'flying' above the entrance, assorted carrier pigeons and some delightful *papier mâché* artworks on a postal theme, often including dogs, every postman's nemesis. Bare girders, peeling woodwork and mosaic

An Austin Morris Royal Mail van provides an unusual snug for customers at the Jolly Postie – the former Royston post office.

floor tiling hint at the structure's utilitarian past and there is an open kitchen complete with a stone cased pizza oven. The bar counter has four hand-pumps, all serving McMullen ales including AK, IPA and the house beer Jolly Postie (ABV 3.8%). Food is important here, with pizza, pasta, burgers and chargrilled meats featuring strongly, and breakfast is served. Booking advisable on Friday/Saturday nights. Judging by my visit, the Postie seems to get customers' stamp of approval.

By boot: Royston's history is linked to its position at the junction of two ancient thoroughfares. There are even mysterious caves in the town centre and the pub is on the site of a medieval hospital. A walking trail is available from the library, museum or online (www.thelistingmagazine.co.uk/royston-town-trail).

ST. ALBANS, HERTFORDSHIRE

Octagonal, timber-framed and once a pigeon house
Ye Olde Fighting Cocks, 16 Abbey Mill Lane, AL3 4HE.
Tel. 01727 869152. www.yeoldefightingcocks.co.uk

A contender among pubs claiming to be the oldest in the country, it is said there has been a beer house on this site since the late eighth century. The timber-framed building dates from *circa* 1485. It was originally a pigeon house, re-erected and adapted for human habitation between 1600-22 by a Thomas Preston. It was called the Three Pigeons in 1750, known as the Round House by the early nineteenth century and renamed the Three Fighting Cocks in a guide book of 1860. The octagonal shape is unique for a pub. Though the structure has been extended several times, the original angular shape can be appreciated inside, where large oak beams provide vertical and horizontal support and angular, sagging ceilings are almost claustrophobically low. A wood fire blazes in winter and there is a bread oven. Archaeologists are puzzled by the fact that the cellar, thought to be the footings for an earlier monastic building, is the same unusual shape as the current one. The

1940s' postcard of Ye Olde Fighting Cocks.

Ye Olde Fighting Cocks, St Albans, was adapted from a pigeon house, which may explain its octagonal shape.

setting is delightful, adjacent to a river and Verulamium Park and lake, with St Albans Abbey a few minutes' walk away. There are two bars and seven ales were on hand-pump when visited, including Purity Ubu, Rebellion IPA, Paradigm Urban Dusk and Haresfoot Wild Boy. Pub branded souvenirs are on sale. Popular with tourists and with a good menu, it's advisable to book if you wish to dine on Sundays or during holiday periods. Dog friendly; outside seating; parking limited.

By boot: A 3-mile city trail linking places of interest is available from the local tourist office or www.enjoystalbans.com. *By bike:* The start of the Alban Way (NCN Route 61), a trail along a former Great Northern Railway line (St Albans-Hatfield) is nearby.

ST. DOGMAELS, PEMBROKESHIRE

Riverside pub where walkers mark end of 186-mile trek

Ferry Inn, Poppit Road, near Cardigan, SA43 3LF.
Tel. 01239 615172. www.ferry-inn.co.uk

This much extended former fisherman's cottage is in a breathtaking location beside the wide Afon Teifi, flowing serenely along lush, wooded banks. Whether you choose to sit inside or outside (on tiered wooden decks and balconies) the views are delightful. The oldest part is the bar, set in the stone-built cottage with low ceilings, comfortable sofas and compact bar counter. There are four hand-pumps serving beers from Cardiff brewer Brains, including SA, Gold and Reverend James. The newer and larger part of the establishment is on several levels, including a dedicated dining area, with slate and wood floors and panoramic windows. The menu is wide-ranging, using mainly local produce including cheeses and specialities such as Ferry Fish Pie with laverbread (seaweed) – booking advised. It is a popular place for walkers celebrating completion of the 186-mile Pembrokeshire Coast Path, which traditionally involves negotiating a path behind the pub inaccessible at high tide. Those who have done the whole walk can obtain a National Trail Certificate marking their achievement at the bar. Ambient music; dog friendly.

By boot: The original route of the Pembrokeshire Coast Path National Trail from/to Amroth starts/finishes here,

View of the Afon Teifi from the Ferry Inn, St Dogmaels. Walkers completing the Pembrokeshire Coast Path can obtain a certificate at the bar.

passing through the pub's gate and behind the building at the water's edge. In 2012 it became part of the Wales Coast Path, the first uninterrupted route along any entire national coast. *By bike:* Just off NCN Route 82 Aberystwyth-Fishguard. *By boat:* The pub has its own jetty.

ST MARY HOO, KENT

A zoo and miniature railway

The Fenn Bell Inn, Allhallows Road, Fenn Street, ME3 8RF.
Tel. 01634 270422. www.fennbellinn.co.uk

Who is watching who? A coati, normally found in the forests of Central America, ambles around its enclosure while a family of meerkats peers curiously at me quaffing a pint of Shepherd Neame Spitfire. Screeches and calls from assorted parrots, macaws and other colourful birds emanate from a spacious aviary. Drinkers and diners soak up the sun at nearby tables,

Customers outside the Fenn Bell Inn view the pub's aviary of exotic birds. There are also meerkats and other animals, along with a ride-on miniature railway.

enjoying this most unexpected pub garden. The Fenn Bell is a red-tiled, part weather-boarded old pub, with a sturdy barn and large garden, on the edge of the Kent marshes. That's where the ordinariness ends as, in 2016, it was granted planning permission for a zoo housing a collection of rescued and exotic animals. It has become popular with parents and grandparents looking for a pub with 'kiddie appeal'. I found the grounds laid out with neat borders, patios and a pergola under which a family party was underway. At the time of my visit a 7¼-inch gauge miniature railway, with a 300-yard loop line and two-platform terminus, was under construction. Completion, and steam haulage, was planned for 2017. Real ales from Kent brewer Shepherd Neame; meals served. Closed Monday/Tuesday except public holidays.

By boot: Within twelve minutes' walk of the Saxon Shore Way where it meets the A228 at Fenn Farm. This 163-mile path follows the coast of East Sussex and Kent. *By bike:* A few minutes' north-east of NCN Route 179, which makes a loop of the Hoo Peninsula and connects with NCN Route 1.

SHEERNESS-ON-SEA, KENT

Grotto built from shipwreck salvage
Ship on Shore, 155 Marine Parade, ME12 2BX.
Tel. 01795 662880.

Attached to this single-storey pub, protected by a towering sea wall, is a structure that resembles a ruined medieval fortress. Closer examination reveals an elaborate folly made from assorted rocks, mortar and curved cement blocks. An exhibit in the bar tells its curious story. A small vessel, the *Lucky Escape*, foundered offshore in 1848, during a northerly gale. Local coastguards recovered its cargo of cement barrels and used them, and an assortment of rocks, to build themselves a shelter next to what then was a simple beer house. They crowned their structure with the ship's figurehead, which no longer survives. When a weather-boarded pub was built on the site it was given its current name. Its unusual appendage became something of a tourist attraction, appearing on numerous postcards and countless holiday snaps. The Grade II-listed building is now

The grotto of the Ship on Shore, Sheerness-on-Sea, depicted on a postcard dated 1913. Servicemen are among the customers. Note the ship's figurehead decorating the roof.

The Ship on Shore. Today's pub is a more substantial one than that glimpsed on the postcard. The grotto's arches have been enclosed.

used as a store room; customers entering the gents' toilet can see a part. The pub's long and narrow main bar, with an area for darts at one end and a conservatory for diners at the other, is decorated with maritime artefacts. There is a wood-panelled bar counter with three hand-pumps, though my pint of Sharp's Doom Bar was served from the cask. Meals are available at lunchtime. Ambient music.

By boot and bike: The sea wall, adjacent to the pub, forms part of the 6-mile Sheerness Way circular route, mainly traffic-free and perfect for families.

SITTINGBOURNE, KENT

Courthouse with prison cells

The Golden Hope, 1 Park Road, ME10 1DR.
Tel. 01795 476791. www.jdwetherspoon.com

Confined to a cell, drinking a pint of Orkney Dragonhead Stout, many questions came to mind. What kind of characters once occupied this cramped space, with its bars, brick walls and six-inch square hatch? What sort of stories could they tell? Were they ever able to select a drink from eight varieties of real ale to accompany their porridge, as I had done? Joking aside, I

Soft cell: An austere brick corridor in the Golden Hope, Sittingbourne. Three prison cells, now converted to cosy snugs, lead off it. The bar occupies the main courtroom of the former Magistrate's Court.

was enjoying lunch with my daughter in one of three vaulted cells that are now secluded snugs, reached via an austere brick corridor. Sittingbourne's former Magistrate's Court and first police station, built in 1856, opened in 2015 as one of the J.D. Wetherspoon chain's commendable conversions of historic buildings. Several former magistrates attended the opening ceremony. The labyrinthine building features exposed brickwork, some original windows and artwork on a penal theme, as well as works on sailing ships (the pub is named after a sea-going barge) and the town's papermaking industry. A long bar counter occupies the former main courtroom, with its heavy beams and unusual lantern tower, and there is hotel accommodation upstairs. There are two patio beer gardens. Meals are served all day.

By boot: The town is situated on the Saxon Shore Way, a 160-mile coastal trail from Gravesend to Hastings. *By bike:* On NCN Route 1 (Dover-Shetlands).

SOURTON, DEVON

An Aladdin's Cave of curios

The Highwayman Inn, near Okehampton, EX20 4HN.
Tel. 01837 861243. www.thehighwaymaninn.net

Drivers on the A386 between Tavistock and Okehampton can't fail to miss this place. The exterior of the rugged stone building, with Gothic windows, has statues of a dragon and rampant horse on the roof, while the former Launceston to Tavistock stage coach forms part of the entrance porch. Just for good measure, a full-size structure resembling the house of the 'old woman who lives in a shoe' (of nursery rhyme fame) forms part of one of the wings, while another fairy tale house stands in the garden, near a rusty water-wheel. The interior, with its rough stone walls and floors,

Staged entrance: The old Launceston – Tavistock stage coach is built into the entrance of the Highwayman Inn. There are many more surprises inside this Gothic-style pub.

is even more surprising, a central hallway leading to two main bars, each with oak beams, snugs, grottoes and Jacobean-style furniture. A 'secret passage' leads to the Locker Bar, resembling the bows of a wooden ship. Assorted memorabilia ranges from horse bridles and pewter tankards to representations of animals in various materials, and a 'tree of possibilities'. Mood lighting comes mainly from *faux* oil lamps augmented by natural light from stained glass windows. A cheese press and air bellows have been transformed into quirky tables, while a tree root forms part of the bar counter. The building has a long history, its role as an inn dating back hundreds of years. In the seventeenth century, it was called the Golden Fleece; Plymouth Breweries later renamed it the New Inn, while work on the curious features seen today began with new landlords in 1959, when it was given its current name. One real ale was available on my visit, Wychwood Hobgoblin, as was local scrumpy cider. Lunchtime food includes organic, vegan and vegetarian options and ranges from a wide range of oggies (pasties) to meat, cheese, and salmon platters, soup and pies. Ambient music; regular events. Access to gents' toilet is from the outside. Accommodation available. Closes for a few hours in the afternoon.

By bike and boot: **The largely traffic-free Granite Way from Okehampton to Lydford, part of the Devon coast-to-coast NCN Route 27, runs through Sourton. It is built on a former Southern Railway line, crossing the spectacular Meldon Viaduct.**

SOUTH SHIELDS, TYNE AND WEAR

Cave bar in a cliff

Marsden Grotto, Coast Road, NE34 7BS.
Tel. 0191 455 6060

This cave bar, excavated from the limestone cliffs, can be reached by lift from road level, via a long, zigzag staircase or directly from the beach. There is a terrace beside the beach and a dining area upstairs. Once a cave dwelling, it was enlarged

Vintage postcard of the Marsden Grotto, with the cliffs rising behind.

The Marsden Grotto today, showing the lift shaft, built in 1938, that allows access to this 'cave pub' from road level.

and made into a pub in the nineteenth century. After a rock fall in the 1860s, protective retaining walls were built. It was owned by Vaux Brewery for a hundred years from the 1890s – the company installed the lift in 1938 – but has since changed hands numerous times. It is said to be haunted by a smuggler murdered by his compatriots for selling out to the revenue men. One landlord reputedly often left a tankard of ale out for the ghost as a peace offering.

By bike: South Shields is at the eastern end of the 174-mile Hadrian's Cycleway to Ravenglass, Cumbria (NCN Route 72).

STOCKPORT, GREATER MANCHESTER

Snug hidden behind the bar

The Arden Arms, 23 Millgate, SK1 2LX.
Tel. 0161 480 2185. www.arden-arms.co.uk

This pub has a very special room: a cosy snug behind the bar. Entering this inner sanctum is not for the self-conscious. All eyes were on my friends and me, since it is polite to ask first, as one has to walk through the serving area and past the beer taps to get there. Customers who make this effort enjoy 'table service' as, paradoxically, they can't easily get to the bar. Only a handful of pubs have a room for customers behind a bar (see Bridge Inn, Topsham, page 127). This one is enhanced with upholstered bench seating and bell-pushes for service, sadly no longer in use. There is also an antique table with a bell-push in the centre which served the same purpose. The nineteenth-century, brick-built former coaching inn is Grade II listed and on CAMRA's National Inventory of historic interiors. The bar has a glazed wooden screen stretching from floor to ceiling, fitted with sash windows so sections can be closed off. There are three other rooms, including the Millgate Room, used for dining. Quarry tiled floors, real fires, wood-panelled walls, a grandfather clock and hand-pumps fixed on the bar-back rather than on the counter are other notable features. Six ales were

View from the bar at the Arden Arms, showing the snug that can only be accessed by passing through the serving area.

garden beside the Grand Union Canal at the bottom of the Stockton lock flight. During the festive season, it comes into its own. I was waiting outside before opening time one evening and it was like enjoying a private *son et lumiere*. A Merry Christmas sign on the wall flashed into life, then two Christmas trees made entirely of lights and topped with shining stars lit up, followed by lights along the eaves and other illuminated features on the wall of an adjacent building. Entering was like walking onto the film set of *Santa Claus – The Movie*. A long main room, with its snugs and oak beams, was filled with fairy lights, tinsel, bells and ribbons. There was a 'winter wonderland' scene with snowmen and snow covered houses, a toy shop window full of old fashioned toys and a fireplace given over to Father Christmas flying on his sleigh through an icy woodland diorama. Somewhere among all this glitz was the bar, its hand-pumps topped with Santa hats.

available, including a Porter (ABV 5.3%), all from Stockport's own Robinson's Brewery. Meals at lunchtimes and some evenings. Outdoor seating in stable courtyard.

By boot: An Ale Trail of Stockport town centre provides some excellent pubs and beers and is highly recommended. Visit the tourist office or online (www.stockport.gov.uk). *By bike:* The Trans Pennine Trail, NCN Route 62 (Fleetwood-Selby) passes through the town.

STOCKTON, WARWICKSHIRE

Canal-side Christmas delight

The Blue Lias, Stockton Road, CV47 8LD.
Tel. 01926 812249. www.bluelias.com

Christmas only comes once a year but at the Blue Lias it lasts the whole of December. The festive decorations for which it is locally renowned are so numerous that staff begin putting them up in November and work as hard as Santa's elves to complete the job. At any time of year this is a delightful place, with a

The Blue Lias decorated for Christmas. Its exterior is equally colourful during the festive season.

A Christmas menu is served through much of December (booking advised). Three real ales were available on my visit – Adnams Broadside, Greene King Abbot and Hook Norton's Greedy Goose. Blue Lias is a purplish limestone found in the area and used in the production of cement. A Stone Age dinosaur features on the pub sign. Private fishing, day tickets sold; camping adjacent.

By boot: A 5-mile circular walk, incorporating the towpath, lock flight and a section of the 100-mile Millennium Way starts from the pub (http://walking.41club.org/ShortLias.htm). *By bike:* On NCN Route 41 (Gloucester-Rugby). *By boat:* Moor near bridge 23.

SUNDERLAND, TYNE AND WEAR

A ceramic delight

Mountain Daisy, 150 Hylton Road, Millfield, SR4 7NX. Tel. 07563 171700. www.mountaindaisy.co.uk

An imposing, three-storey former hotel rebuilt in the early 1900s. The main bar is at the front but I found a hidden gem behind a locked door: the spectacular Buffet Bar. The landlord was happy to open up on request, revealing one of the most beautiful bars I have seen. It has tiling which extends to the walls, floor and around the front of a curving, marble-topped bar counter. The highlight is seven large ceramic framed murals by Craven Dunnill & Co. of Shropshire, depicting scenic views of north-east England. They show the High Bridge at Newcastle, Durham Cathedral on its rocky crag, Wearmouth Bridge, Sunderland, the ruins of Finchale Abbey (pronounced finkle) beside the River Wear, Marsden Rock at South Shields, Bamburgh Castle and the historic house of Cragside. The floor is a decorative mosaic and the windows contain three stained glass depictions of Jacobean gentlemen enjoying drink, tobacco and the hunt. There is an Art Nouveau floral fire surround, ceramic coving around the ceiling and upholstered bench

Buffet Bar at the Mountain Daisy, Sunderland, showing the marble-topped counter and three of the seven ceramic murals of beauty-spots, by Craven Dunnill & Co.

seating. One real ale, Robinson's Trooper, was available on my visit. There is a function room with period fittings upstairs. On CAMRA's National Inventory.

By bike: West of NCN Route 1 (Dover-Shetlands).

SWANSEA, WEST GLAMORGAN

Historic wine store where Dylan Thomas supped

No Sign Bar, 56 Wind Street, SA1 1EG. Tel. 01792 465300. www.nosignwinebar.com

It's not just the name that's unusual here. The long, narrow hostelry was previously a brewery but became a wine merchants in the 1830s. Despite having a bar and tasting room it wasn't classed as a public house and therefore didn't require an inn sign. Poet Dylan Thomas was a regular customer. He called it the Wine Vaults, and the adjacent Salubrious Passage (from where access was once possible) became Paradise Passage in his

The front room of Swansea's No Sign Bar still has the look of a Victorian wine shop. A portrait of wine merchant William Clark hangs above the fireplace.

short story *The Followers*. The front room still has the look of a Victorian wine shop, being lined with glazed display cabinets and a portrait of wine merchant William Clark (d. 1875). Walking through the building you pass a glazed screen, two bar counters and a seating area with pitched roof. These were previously separate rooms. The floor is a composite of wood and slate and there are cast-iron pillars supporting the ceiling. There are old bills of sale and catalogues relating to the bar's previous incarnation. Downstairs, cavernous and vaulted wine cellars, named appropriately The Vault – used for live music at weekends – are supported by iron columns. A rail-mounted gantry crane, once used for shifting wine vats and casks of port and sherry, sits motionless beneath the ceiling. There is also an upstairs cocktail bar and outside terrace and downstairs, a portrait of Dylan Thomas looking over the long-gone Mumbles Railway. Four ales were available, including Purple Moose Dark Side of the Moose, Mumbles' Oystermouth Stout and a very

hoppy One Inch Punch from Newport's Tiny Rebel. A wide-ranging menu is served. Ambient music.

By bike: The Celtic Trail, part of NCN Route 4 (London-Fishguard) passes nearby. A traffic-free cycle path following Swansea Bay to Mumbles Head is a scenic ride along the former Mumbles Railway trackbed.

THAME, OXFORDSHIRE

Former prison and leper house
The Birdcage, 4 Cornmarket, OX9 3DX. Tel. 01844 217911. www.birdcagepub.co.uk

This market town's oldest pub, the Birdcage is the name of the building it occupies, dating back 700 years. It has served variously as a prison, armoury and leper-house. Reputedly haunted, I spoke with a barmaid who has experienced doors opening without human intervention and the sound of footsteps on the stairs when no-one was there. The landlord joined our conversation, telling me he had heard a glass fly off a table and smash against a wall, though no customers (clumsy or otherwise) were around at the time. With its 'layer-cake' of jettied upper storeys, the timber-framed structure presents a veritable forest of beams, inside and out. Combined with its wooden floors, the edifice must creak and groan like a man o'war during a storm. Oriel windows with leaded glass panes, 'dragon beams' of elm and, inside, aumbries (wall recesses for religious artefacts) add to the unique look.

The building probably started as an administration centre for the town's market, which was granted by Royal Charter: it's a landmark on the wide, long main street. It is likely that the cellar, the oldest part of the structure, was a lock-up (cage) for arms, armour and local petty offenders from earliest times. Lepers were kept, out of public gaze, on the upper storey. Records state that, *circa* 1600, the property was held by a yeoman named Philip Bird – when it may first have been known as Bird's Cage. From 1805, during the Napoleonic wars,

The 700 year-old Birdcage in Thame is a forest of beams, inside and out.

Edwardian view of the Bird Cage Inn when it was owned by Simonds Brewery of Reading. The stucco was removed by the brewery in 1948.

16 French prisoners were incarcerated in the cellar (it was common for all large towns to house their share of POWs). The prisoners must have had certain freedoms, as you'll deduce on visiting Thame Museum. An exhibit there is a portrait of Penelope Loader, the illegitimate daughter of Penelope Turner and 'a French prisoner resident in the Birdcage.' Meanwhile, a former landlady, Pat Ellis, claimed to have encountered a 'restless soul' on the top floor, whom she believed was the ghost of a leper who had been stoned to death. It is likely the Birdcage's role as an inn started in the late fifteenth century. It was in the ownership of brewers from the late nineteenth,

changing hands from Watlington Brewery to Simonds Brewery of Reading in 1906. There is seating in nooks and crannies and a separate dining area. Drinks include more than a hundred bottled craft and speciality beers and ciders. Two cask ales from Marlow's Rebellion brewery were served on my visit, IPA and Smugglers. Food served; ambient music; outside seating.

By boot: **Thame has a variety of good pubs and is ideal for a pub crawl.** *By bike:* **NCN Route 57, the traffic-free Phoenix Trail on a former railway from Princes Risborough, passes nearby and continues to Oxford.**

TOPSHAM, DEVON

Bar is the landlady's front parlour— the Queen has called in for tea

The Bridge Inn, Bridge Hill, near Exeter, EX3 0QQ.
Tel. 01392 873862. www.cheffers.co.uk/bridge.html

This former brewery dates from the sixteenth century and the inn has been in the same family since the 1890s. In 1998, on the occasion of the Cheffers family's 101 years of ownership, the pub was honoured by a visit from HM Queen Elizabeth II. Her Majesty was presented with a case of ale brewed for the occasion by Branscombe Vale Brewery. The pink-and-black jumble of tile-hung buildings stands near the River Clyst and an ancient stone bridge which crosses it. The interior, unchanged for decades, is more a family home than a pub and is furnished accordingly. In a series of rooms and snugs off the wood-panelled hallway are a grandfather clock, a stone fireplace, high-

Parlour of the Bridge Inn, Topsham, which doubles as a servery: customers can sit there on request. The cellar is seen through the doorway and this has a serving hatch for people in the garden.

backed settles and historical family photographs. A sign on a door indicates that this is the landlady's front parlour, an inner-sanctum where customers may sit on request. Another sign, from an earlier age, states 'this room is prohibited from all amusements on Sunday. W.G. Gibbings, Proprietor'. Amusements are now permitted, with the exception of mobile phones and other electronic devices, which a notice advises must be switched off. A few steps separate the parlour from the cellar, where a variety of mainly local ales – Exeter, Otter, Exe Valley and Branscombe Vale on my visit – were available from cask. There's local cider, too. An adjoining former maltings contains another bar, used for special occasions, and this is filled with assorted furniture and memorabilia. Outdoor serving hatch. Outdoor seating adjacent to river; lunchtime food; dog friendly.

By boot and bike: Topsham is on a largely traffic-free 15-mile trail from Exeter to Turf Lock (see also Turf Hotel page 58). NCN Route 2. *By boat:* There is a seasonal ferry linking Topsham with Turf Lock.

TUNBRIDGE WELLS, KENT

Opera is still staged

The Opera House, 86 Mount Pleasant Road, TN1 1RT.
Tel. 01892 511770. www.jdwetherspoon.com

'A night at the opera' takes on a whole new meaning at this sumptuous public house. Built in 1902 in Neo-Georgian style, with a Baroque domed centrepiece to designs by John Briggs, its opera house era was short. Turned into a cinema in 1931, an unexploded World War II bomb caused a fire which stopped screenings until 1949. The decline continued when it became a bingo hall in the 1960s. Transition to one of the country's most grand pubs came in 1997, opening as part of the J.D. Wetherspoon chain. The interior has been sensitively restored, including the foyer and auditorium with its two curved balconies and eight private boxes. The Dress Circle retains its tip-up

Postcard of the Opera House in 1909, when it was still used as such, showing passers-by (two carrying parasols).

seating and glazed screen, complete with lily decoration, while the ceiling is richly detailed. The stage now incorporates seating as well as one of the two bar counters. Look carefully and you'll see the flytower retains its scenery winch and metal hooks. There are the weights for the curtain mechanism and a complicated electrical control panel high above the stage. The pub has a certain genteel ambience as befitting its heritage; even conversation seems to be carried on in hushed tones and there is no ambient music. There is a good real ale offering which, when I called, included guests from Mordue, Long Man, Acorn, Dark

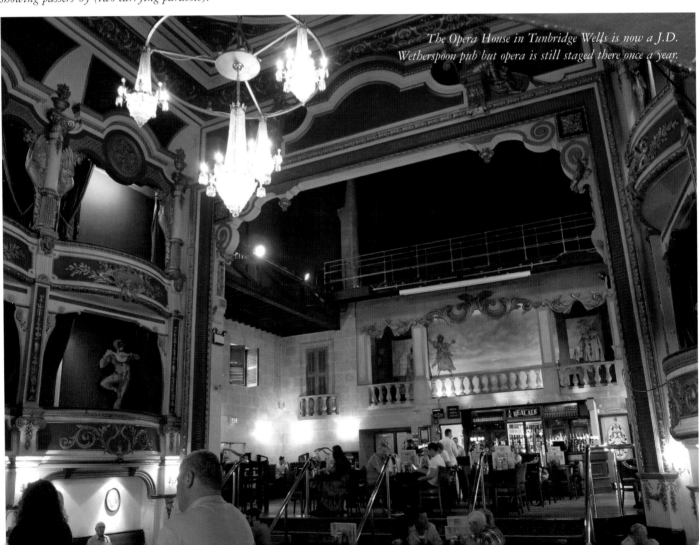

The Opera House in Tunbridge Wells is now a J.D. Wetherspoon pub but opera is still staged there once a year.

Star and Wadworths. Once a year the establishment returns to its theatrical roots: tickets are sold including for the boxes and upper tiers, and operas are staged. Meals served all day.

By boot: **The Weald Way passes through the town on its 80-mile route across the North and South Downs and through the Weald of Kent, linking the Thames with Eastbourne.** *By bike:* **The High Weald Ride, NCN Route 18 to Canterbury, starts in town.**

WAKEFIELD, WEST YORKSHIRE

Most gas lights in a pub

The King's Arms, Heath Common, Heath, WF1 5SL.
Tel. 01924 377527. www.thekingsarmsheath.co.uk

I was lucky to visit on a cold and gloomy January day. With possibly the largest number of working gas lamps of any UK pub (according to CAMRA) and several real fires blazing, this is a place that comes into its own in winter. I counted more than 30 lamps hissing and glowing in the maze of rooms that include

The King's Arms, near Wakefield, developed from eighteenth-century cottages. Gas-lit, there are other delightful period features.

a flag-stoned snug, wood-panelled front bar and another with a working range. The oak-beamed hostelry was developed from eighteenth-century cottages in the 1840s and has slowly expanded to include former stables and a large, modern conservatory. Even that is gas-lit. Diners were numerous, but I felt equally at home just sampling the choice of real ales from West Yorkshire's Ossett Brewery, including the eponymous house bitter and ales from Fernandes, Liverpool Organic, Riverhead and Clark's. The stone-built pub sits at the edge of a common surrounded by buildings dating from the fifteenth century. A contrast with the ring-roads and retail sheds of Wakefield, a short bus ride away. On CAMRA's National Inventory. Large garden; dog friendly; no ambient music.

By boot: **A leaflet of walks from Heath Common has been produced by Wakefield District Council (www.wakefield.gov.uk).** *By bike:* **NCN Route 67, the Transpennine Trail, passes Heath Common between Wakefield and Barnsley.**

Every man's dream shed

Wakefield Labour Club (aka The Red Shed),
18 Vicarage Street, WF1 1QX. Tel. 01924 215626.
www.theredshed.org.uk

A cosy shed that doubles as a pub, nicely decorated and stocked with draught beer, set at the end of your garden, has to be the ultimate male fantasy. Imagine popping out of your back door to enjoy an ever-changing choice of real ales, a selection of bottled Belgian beers and even a regular gig by live bands. A dream come true! The Red Shed has all this, except it is not in a domestic garden but marooned in the middle of a busy town centre, in the shadow of a towering shopping mall. Despite its central location and pillar-box colour, I had a job finding the place. It involved asking lots of people, being directed around the labyrinthine Trinity Walk shopping centre, taking a lift near Debenhams to a side exit and crossing a car park. But the trek was worth it: this is a friendly oasis for conversation and

The Red Shed in Wakefield, a haven for real ale. It has its own anthem, sung to the tune of The Red Flag.

well-kept beer. Seven ales were available on my visit: I enjoyed a Roosters Yankee and Moorhouses Blonde Witch. The shed was military surplus (reputedly relocated from Aldershot), cost £400 and was opened in 1966. If it looks somewhat out-of-place beneath a modern department store, this is because it was saved from demolition during the redevelopment of the city's old market area. A small bar, simply furnished, leads to a larger room where live music is staged and, occasionally, speakers hold forth. They have included such luminaries as Vanessa Redgrave, Tony Benn and John Prescott. It became headquarters for the local miners' support group during the 1980s' miners' strike. A band was rehearsing during my visit. Other diversions include a library stocking titles such as *Utopianism and Marxism* and *Democracy Today and Tomorrow,* and a television but no ambient music. I was told the local MP and councillors are regulars, but people of all, or no, political persuasions are welcome. The anthem, displayed among other memorabilia on the wall, is clearly partisan and sung to the tune of *The Red Flag:* '... while Tories scoff and Liberals sneer, we'll keep the Red Shed standing here.' Open evenings only except Saturday (all day).

While in Wakefield: Don't miss the Fernandes Brewery Tap. Hidden down a side lane off the main thoroughfare, the upper floor of this Ossett Brewery house and the Fernandes micro-brewery doubles as a gallery of lost pub signs. I counted thirteen – from the Black Bull to the Tally Ho, from the Prince of Wales to the Duke of Devonshire – displayed in a wood-beamed bar serving a variety of ales. The lower floor is a continental style bier keller with regular live music. 5 Avison Yard, Wakefield, WF1 1UA. Tel. 01924 386348. www.ossett-brewery.co.uk.

By boat: The Aire and Calder Navigation is twelve minutes' walk south of the Red Shed.

WALLSEND, TYNE AND WEAR

Art deco cinema – and a 'see through' beer cellar
The Ritz, 87-93 High Street West, NE28 8JD.
Tel. 01912 969600. www.jdwetherspoon.co.uk

The Ritz is a cinema conversion in Wallsend, a town where Get Carter! *starring Michael Caine was filmed.*

Built as a cinema in the Art Deco style, the building was restored and opened as a pub by J.D. Wetherspoon in 2015 at a cost of £1.26 million. The 1600-seater picture-house had lain empty and unused for four years after almost fifty years as a Mecca bingo hall. The entrance is theatrical, a façade of stone and brick with cast-iron decoration, then a plant-filled loggia to a spacious bar. An interesting feature, not seen in any other pub I have visited, is a ground floor cellar with viewing panels so customers can see the beer casks and associated paraphernalia through glass. In fact, the whole pub is on the ground floor, including a snug and a gilt-effect false ceiling in the former auditorium. This is equipped with a dazzling and varied display of *deco*-style lighting. A marble-topped bar counter contains 12 hand-pumps dispensing a wide range of ales. I enjoyed the spicy, floral taste of Mordue's Admiral (ABV 4.8%). There's an open kitchen at one end of the bar and a large outside patio. Artwork by local artists includes a spherical steel sculpture representing the Tyneside shipbuilding industry of Wallsend. RMS *Mauretania*, the largest vessel in the world at the time, was built here. The cinema was designed by Percy L. Browne as part of the ABC chain and opened in 1939 with *Gangster's Boy* and *Lassie from Lancashire* and screened its final film in 1962. Other claims to fame are that rock star Sting was born in Wallsend and the film *Get Carter!* starring Michael Caine was made there, though it is not known if the actor visited this cinema.

By boot: Wallsend is at the eastern end of the Hadrian's Wall National Trail. **By bike:** The Hadrian's Cycleway (NCN Route 72) is to the south, following the Tyne.

WALSALL, WEST MIDLANDS

'Queasy floor' with 'shallow' and 'deep' ends
White Lion, 150 Sandwell Street, WS1 3EQ.
www.admiraltaverns.co.uk

I didn't know before visiting that *Three Men in a Boat* author and inveterate pub-goer Jerome K. Jerome's birthplace is in

Doors are marked 'shallow end' and 'deep end' in Walsall's White Lion, due to the pub's sloping floor.

Walsall; nor that one of the first CAMRA branches was established in town. This rather grand, late-Victorian community local, with its moulded stone door frames, semi-elliptical windows and half-timbered gables, holds another surprise. Close observation reveals it is built on a slope: something that became more apparent as I entered the 'L' shaped public bar. The landlord told me the floor level varies by 3 feet from one end to the other. It can seem disorientating, especially after a pint or two, which is why it is sometimes known as the 'queasy floor'. To aid navigation, interior doors are marked 'deep end' and 'shallow end.' The staff have to get used to constantly walking up and down hill – though the cellar has a slightly gentler gradient. The darts area has a specially-built oche floor, making it level for players. Green leather bench seating lines the walls; there's a piano and, above it, historic photos of the town. There were four ales available, including two from Wye Valley and one each from Adnams and Purple

Moose. There is also a lounge and garden. Dog friendly; regular live music.

By bike: Situated west of NCN Route 5 (Reading-Holyhead).

WEST BOLDON, TYNE AND WEAR

Quirky memorabilia and photo gallery
The Black Horse, Rectory Bank, NE36 0QQ. Tel. 0191 536 1814.

An antique commode, a 1960s' women's hairdryer, a steak and kidney pie dispenser and an African tribal drum are some of the more unusual items on display here. When I add a reel-to-reel tape recorder, a television still showing programmes from half a century ago, assorted typewriters, hats and vintage radios to the list, you will realise that someone has the collecting bug. That someone is Pete 'Zulu' Robson, founder member of punk band the Toy Dolls (best known for their 1982 version of children's

Cosy corner of the Black Horse, West Boldon, which contains an eclectic range of memorabilia.

song *Nellie the Elephant*), who is also chef-proprietor. Candles and retro lampshades are used to light the exhibits and there is a gallery of Mr Robson's black-and-white photos. The L-shaped bar features a snug at one end and a restaurant at the other, with soft furnishings and blazing fires contributing to a cosy feel. There were two real ales, from Titanic and Jennings, on my visit. This is a dining pub, whose menu includes daily specials: booking is advised. The menus are contained within old LP covers; others can be seen on the walls. Some of the tables are decorated with photographs and *Vogue* magazine covers. Ambient music; beer garden; regular live music.

By boot: **The River Don walk follows its waters to West Boldon from the River Tyne at Jarrow.** *By bike:* **The 12-mile Bede's Way Trail (NCN Route 14) passes through nearby East Boldon, on its way from Monkwearmouth to Jarrow.**

WROXHAM, NORFOLK

A boat house
The Boat Shed, The Peninsular, Staitheway Road, NR12 8TH. Tel. 01603 783892. www.boatshedwroxham.co.uk

It calls itself 'the best kept secret on the Broads'. Look at the walking instructions on the pub's website and you'll realise why. A cryptic series of directions involves crossing a car park, going through a gate and barrier, turning at a green crane and following an arrow. At the end of this zigzag route is a large boat shed, holiday cruisers moored outside. There's no inn sign, in fact no indication this is a pub at all until I entered to find a spacious room filled with customers and the buzz of conversation. The building's previous roles included leisure centre and café before its present incarnation in 2009. The wooden floor is suspended above the water where boats once rested. This may explain its gentle slope and the reason there is a cooled area for ale storage rather than a cellar. Shiplapped walls, beams covered with myriad pump-clips and a mixture of

Ship-shape: From the outside it looks like a typical boat house, but the Boat Shed is a busy pub. It serves up to 14 ales and hosts regular live music.

armchairs, sofas and rustic tables and chairs give an informal feel. There is a snooker area, dartboard and a variety of maritime photographs and fishing rods on display. It is a joy to look outside and see boats bobbing on the water – there's outside seating too. Black Sheep and Sharp's Doom Bar are the regular ales on hand-pump, with up to 12 more ales served from the cask (five on my visit, including Woodforde's Nelson's Revenge and honey-infused Bumble Beer from Wentworth, South Yorkshire). There's also a selection of ciders. Live music and karaoke sessions are part of an events programme. Meals and ice-cream served; dog friendly. Of interest to ale fans: Woodforde's Brewery and visitor centre is 4 miles to the south-east.

By boot: The 9-mile Bure Valley footpath follows the eponymous narrow-gauge railway to Aylsham. *By bike:* Broads Circular Route 9 via Horning and Ludham – see www.thebroadsbybike.org.uk. Also, the above Bure Valley path can be cycled. *By boat:* Wroxham is a popular base for boating holidays on the Broads; seasonal boat trips are available and day boats can be hired.

YORK, NORTH YORKSHIRE

Time-capsule Edwardian smoke room
Blue Bell, 53 Fossgate, YO1 9TF. Tel. 01904 654904.

Described by CAMRA as a 'national treasure', this is one of a handful of pubs to be Grade II* listed. Yet the red-tiled street frontage is so small, with just one window and door, it is easy to walk straight past. Dating from 1903, the compact interior layout is unchanged, its walls and ceilings lined with varnished wood panels. A narrow corridor, with a glazed drinking lobby, serving hatch and folding wooden seat, leads to the rear Smoke Room. Its title is etched in engraved glass on the door. Fitted upholstered benches line the walls, there are period light fittings, an ornate fire surround and a glazed bar front with a lifting service window. Sitting here with a pint on a quiet winter afternoon, with the fire blazing and one or two locals for company, I found it easy to imagine myself in the Edwardian

The Edwardian Smoke Room of the Blue Bell in York has hardly changed since 1903.

era, when the British Empire was at its zenith. The loss of the *Titanic* and horrors of the Great War lay in the future. The quarry-tiled front bar is also delightful, with its window engraved 'Blue Bell'; a tiled fire surround and a panelled bar counter. Television screens, piped music and games machines are notably absent: this is a place for conversation or contemplation. Edwardian traditions are maintained: 'no swearing, shouting or noisy groups' are the house rules. The time-capsule condition is largely thanks to being run by the same family of licensees for much of the last century. It continues in good hands today. Seven real ales were available, with Yorkshire beers predominating, including examples from Acorn, Roosters, Timothy Taylor, Kelham Island and Rudgate. Real cider; sandwiches served at lunchtime. On CAMRA National Inventory; dog friendly.

By boot: York is a pedestrian friendly city and one of the highlights is a walk around the medieval city walls (approximately 3 miles). All city pubs featured here are within the walls and within easy walking distance of each other. The walls can be walked from 8am until dusk. *By bike:* A bike rental outlet is situated next to the railway station.

The antique furniture in York's Guy Fawkes Inn looks even more eerie by gaslight. One of the beers served is Centurion's Ghost.

Gas-lit and reputedly linked to the Gunpowder Plotter

Guy Fawkes Inn, 25 High Petergate, YO1 7HP.
Tel. 01904 466674.

Dating from *circa* 1700, this town house stands opposite the medieval church where Guy Fawkes was baptised in 1570. Whether the Gunpowder Plot conspirator was born here, as claimed on the window plaques, is debatable, though he was certainly born in the vicinity. An old house behind, part of the inn complex, is called Guy Fawkes Cottage. His mother lived on the site so it is possible he entered the world there. (Fawkes attended nearby St Peter's School and it still refuses to burn his effigy on November 5th.) The inn has bare floorboards and is full of antique furniture, including church pews, decoratively carved benches and a tall pendulum clock. A suit of armour stands in a corner of the front lounge, looking eerie by gaslight. The place is atmospheric after dark, when numerous gas lamps are lit, their warm glow filling the dining room. Gas mantles are in place in other rooms but were not working on my visit. There was a range of five real ales, including York Brewery's Centurion's Ghost, Copper Dragon Golden Pippin, Black Sheep Best Bitter and Timothy Taylor's Boltmaker. There is an extensive menu. Ambient music; accommodation available; patio garden.

By boot: See Blue Bell entry.

England's most flooded pub

King's Arms, 3 King's Staith, YO1 9SN.
Tel. 01904 659435.

About four times a year its staff have to admit defeat, closing the doors to customers and allowing the River Ouse to flow into the pub. The locals have seen it all before and know it won't be long before the King's Arms, converted from a counting house in 1898, is back in business. It has flooded so often that the owners, Tadcaster Brewer Samuel Smith, have adapted the building to cope with the worst Mother Nature can throw at it. The pub can be made 'flood-ready' in half-an-hour and be back in business as little as four hours after waters have subsided. On receiving a flood warning, customers are moved into a back room and a flood gate is locked into position in front of the river-facing door. All fittings, including interior doors and the bar, are designed to be easily dismantled for storage upstairs. The cellar is on an upper level and there's no real ale. Electrical points have been fitted above flood level and the walls and floors are designed to be hosed down, like a big shower room. The

The King's Arms with the River Ouse in flood. The box in the foreground houses heavy-duty drying equipment.

measures were installed after a bad water incursion in 1982 and at least one member of staff usually remains on site. 'The longest I've been stuck here is nine days,' manager Martin Hemstock told the *Morning Advertiser* (16 August, 2007). 'I've got a room full of beer, a catering kitchen and Sky television, it's not all bad. On one occasion a couple canoed in through one door and out the other,' he said. In normal conditions there are riverside tables, chairs and umbrellas outside on the cobbled King's Staith. Inside, a flood level indicator shows how high the water has got over the years. Samuel Smith's beers and products are served.

By boat: **Daily cruises are run during most of the year by York Boat from the adjacent landing.** ***By boot:*** **See page 134.**

Beneath the Roman Bath pub in York are these Roman remains, part of a small museum. The walkway on the right is 4 feet above the street level of AD 300.

A Roman spa in the cellar
Roman Bath, 9 St Sampsons Square, YO1 8RN.
Tel. 01904 620455.

This former coaching inn, in the city centre near The Shambles, was gutted by fire in 1929. As part of the subsequent rebuild, it was decided to enlarge the cellar. Excavations revealed that the Romans had been there first. Part of a Roman bath house, including the *Caldarium* (hot steam room) and *Frigidarium* (cold plunge pool) – a leisure centre used by five thousand soldiers of the legionary fortress of *Eboracum* – was unearthed. These remains, dating from *circa* AD 300, form the heart of a subterranean museum (admission charge) run as an adjunct to the pub. It is reached via cellar steps. A viewing walkway is four feet above the level of the old Roman street. Exhibits include replica military uniforms and sponges on sticks – the Roman version of toilet paper. The pub above is supported on concrete pillars to protect the remains. The bar is one large L-shaped room with decoration on a Roman theme, including replicas of murals, a wall fountain and a larger-than-life statue of a female bath attendant. There is a cabinet of genuine ceramic Roman artefacts; and leaded stained glass windows dating from the 1930s' rebuild. Two real ales were available, John Smith's Cask and Sharp's Doom Bar. Food served; ambient music; regular live music; beer garden; accommodation available.

By boot: **See page 134.**

3. TIPS FOR WALKERS, CYCLISTS AND WATERWAY USERS

EVERY ENTRY IN the Gazetteer contains a full address, but there is in most cases also a post-script titled 'by boot', 'by bike' or 'by boat'. This provides additional information on the pub's location to assist those who enjoy the pursuits of walking, cycling and boating respectively. In some cases, all three options are possible. One doesn't have to drive to get to a pub – in fact, I have found getting there is half the fun. I travelled by car to only a fraction of the hostelries featured. Many were reached using a combination of train travel and walking, or train and cycling. The following notes are designed to be read in conjunction with the pub entries. They are not comprehensive but I hope they are helpful.

The footpath and cycle route across Barmouth Bridge, looking towards the Last Inn (page 120). Inset: Pubs on the Thames Path include The Bounty (page 28).

BY BOOT

Agreeable ambles can be had in towns as well as country. Some of my most enjoyable walks (i.e. pub crawls) have been through the-streets of **Birmingham, Edinburgh, Glasgow, London, Manchester** and **Newcastle upon Tyne** – and not forgetting **Dudley** – usually with like-minded friends. As well as taking a paper Ordnance Survey or street map with me, I usually carry a pocket compass. Digital mapping and GPS direction finding on mobile phones is all very well, but batteries tend to fail at the time you need them most. I'm not an orienteer but a glance at a compass ensures I am walking in the right direction and is an aid if I lose my way. The websites I refer to most when searching for information on footpaths and trails are:

National Trails – the official guide: www.nationaltrail.co.uk
Long Distance Walkers Association: www.ldwa.org.uk
The Ramblers (especially the 'routes and places to walk' section): www.ramblers.org.uk

Among the pubs that I have most enjoyed visiting on foot are those in: **Barmouth** (base for good estuary and hill walks); **Bourne End** (on the Thames Path); **Checkendon** (the Chiltern Hills are delightful); **Dudley**, home of classic Black Country pubs and breweries (combine walking with use of the local bus network); **Geldeston** (try a walk along the valley in one direction from Beccles and return by ferry); **Ilfracombe** and **Combe Martin** (South West Coast Path); **Margate** and **Broadstairs** (the Viking Coastal Trail is a scenic route around Thanet); **Lacock** (National Trust-owned village); **Llanthony** (Offa's Dyke National Trail); **Piel Island** (coastal walk from Barrow-in-Furness); and **St Dogmaels** (Pembrokeshire Coast Path).

Pub walks in cities featured in this book offer a chance to take in a feast of historical and cultural delights as well as unusual pubs. In **London,** for example, you could walk between Ye Olde Cheshire Cheese, the Knights Templar, Ye Olde Mitre and the Black Friar – all featured herein – taking in nearby sights such as the Royal Courts of Justice, Temple Church, Fleet Street and St Paul's Cathedral on the way. In **Chester,** I reached my featured pubs partly using the 2-mile City Walls Trail (its walls are the best preserved of any English city) and partly the Millennium Festival Trail, which takes in 40 historic buildings. Each one has its own plaque, including a few ancient inns. **York,** too, is best explored on foot and has its own walk along the city walls – with enough great pubs to keep you busy for months. **Newcastle upon Tyne's** three featured pubs are also walkable. I particularly enjoyed a stroll along the waterfront between the Hop and Cleaver and the Free Trade Inn, taking in the famous bridges and other sights along the way.

BY BIKE

Why not pedal your way to a pint? You don't have to wear Lycra or ride a designer bike. I have a folding Brompton bicycle that has accompanied me on many leisure trips. Easy to fold and store in a car boot, or on a bus or train (it doesn't require a ticket or pre-booking) I simply unfold it to complete the last stage of my journey or commence a tour. I often take my full-size bicycle on trains too, which requires a little additional planning as there are some restrictions. These mainly relate to Monday to Friday peak hours, when it isn't allowed on commuter trains; and InterCity trains, when booking is usually required for bikes (but there is no charge). Things vary a little between individual train operating companies. For full details and other options, a leaflet titled *Cycling by Train* is available from station ticket offices, or see the PlusBike section of www.nationalrail.co.uk

Sustrans' National Cycling Network (NCN) is excellent. It mostly uses lightly trafficked, or traffic-free thoroughfares and there's excellent mapping on the charity's website, www.sustrans.org.uk. Where appropriate, I have shown the NCN route number(s) closest to the pubs featured. To plan longer tours, or generally to look at the 'bigger picture' on cycling infrastructure in various parts of the country, I have used the fold-out map *UK Cycle Route Planner,* published by Excellent Books. An on-line journey planner specially designed for cyclists can be found at www.cyclestreets.net.

In London, the easily available rental bikes from kerbside docking stations, officially called Santander Cycles but usually referred to as 'Boris bikes', are ideal for short trips. Once you have paid the bike access fee for the day (£2 at the time of writing), the first thirty minutes for each journey is free. Longer journeys cost £2 for each extra thirty minutes. It is easy to plan a low-cost tour with individual 'legs' of less than half-an-hour, to keep costs to a minimum. Information: https://tfl.gov.uk/modes/cycling/santander-cycles. Bicycles can also be taken on board Thames River Bus services (see below).

Among the pubs that I have most enjoyed visiting by bicycle (often as part of a day's general cycling in the area) are those in: **Andover**; **Aston** and **Cholmondeley**, Cheshire; **Bristol**; **Canvey Island**; **Checkendon**; **Exminster** and **Topsham** (Exe Estuary Trail); **Guildford** (Surrey is good cycling country); **Bradford-on-Avon** and **Honey Street** (both on the Kennet & Avon Canal path); **Huish Episcopi** (the Somerset Levels provides easy cycling); those in Kent, particularly in the **Broadstairs** and **Margate** areas (Viking Coastal Trail) and **Dungeness** (nearby Romney Marsh offers good cycling); many of those in inner and outer **London**; and **Portishead** (there's a trail, mainly off-road, linking it with **Bristol**).

BY BOAT

Where pubs can be reached by ferry or public cruises I have noted this. Please check in advance that services are operating. They are seasonal and/or affected by weather conditions. Pubs that are on or near the canal network can be reached by narrow-boat, though they do not always have visitor moorings adjacent. Sometimes, there are public cruises available on the relevant stretch of waterway (which I have noted where known). It is worth considering renting a narrow-boat for a self-drive cruise. No previous experience is necessary – instruction is given – and day boats are available from some local boatyards if you don't want to devote a complete holiday or short break to this enjoyable pastime. Discounts are available to CAMRA members from some boat hire companies, such as CanalCruising.co.uk (01785 813982).

Information on mooring and facilities: www.canalrivertrust.org.uk

In London, there is a system of Thames River Bus services. Five routes operate from 20 piers between Putney and Woolwich and 11 new piers are planned. Services are run by MBNA Thames Clippers. A zonal fares system is in place, like that for buses and the Underground. Website: www.thamesclippers.com

Among the pubs I have most enjoyed visiting by boat (or would do, given half the chance) are those in: **Exminster** (Exeter Canal); **Geldeston** (ferry service from Beccles); **Bourne End** (River Thames); **Cresswell Quay** (Cresswell River); **Bradford-on-Avon** and **Honey Street** (Kennet & Avon Canal); **Banbury** and **Napton** (Oxford Canal); **Nottingham** (Nottingham & Beeston Canal); **Piel Island** (via the Piel Channel ferry); **St Dogmaels** (Afon Teifi); **Stockton**, Warwickshire (Grand Union Canal); **Topsham** (River Clyst); **Wroxham** (Norfolk Broads) and the Black Friar in **London** (Thames River Bus).

BIBLIOGRAPHY

Ainsworth, Paul (Editor), *Real Heritage Pubs of the Midlands,* St Albans, CAMRA, 2015.

Belsey, James, *Heritage Pubs of Great Britain,* St Albans, CAMRA, 1998.

British Film Institute, *Roll Out the Barrel – the British Pub on Film 1944-1982,* (including *Henry Cleans Up,* 1974), double DVD, BFI, 2012.

Brandwood, Geoff, *Britain's Best Real Heritage Pubs,* St Albans, CAMRA, 2013 and 2016.

Brown, Pete, *Man Walks Into a Pub,* Pan Macmillan, 2003 (updated 2010).

Bruning, Ted, *Historic Pubs of London,* Prion Books, 1998.

Clark, Peter, *The English Alehouse – A Social History 1200-1830,* Harlow, Longman, 1983.

Daniel, Guy St John (Rev.), *The Ostrich: Its place in history,* Colnbrook, Ostrich Inn, seventh edition 2005.

Ferguson, Euan, *Drink London – The 100 Best Bars and Pubs,* Frances Lincoln, 2014.

Gamston, David (Editor), *Yorkshire's Real Heritage Pubs,* St Albans, CAMRA, 2011.

King, David (Editor), *The Black Country Good Beer Guide,* St Albans, CAMRA, 2006.

Martin, Brian P., *Tales from the Country Pub,* Newton Abbot, David & Charles, 2001.

McGrath, Gavin, *From Pictures to Pints – Cinemas that became Pubs,* Cinema Theatre Association, 2015.

Mirams, Michael David, *Kent Inns and Inn Signs,* Gillingham, Meresborough Books, 1987.

Moody, Paul (and Turner, Robin), *The Rough Pub Guide,* Orion Books, 2008.

Protz, Roger (Editor), *Good Beer Guide 2013, 2014* St Albans, CAMRA, 2012 and 2013.

Rodwell, Kirsty (and Ferguson Mann Architects), *The George Inn – Norton St. Philip,* Devizes, Wadworth Brewery, 1999.

Russell, Ronald, *Waterside Pubs – Pubs of the Inland Waterways,* Newton Abbot, David & Charles, 1974.

Saxon, Jon (Editor), *Doghouse, the British Pub Magazine,* Issue 3 (Black Country pubs), Ludlow, Son of Saxon, 2012.

Saunders, Chris, *Pints of View (Fighting Cocks, Myth, legend and facts,* 22-23), St Albans, South Herts. CAMRA, December/January 2012 edition.

Slaughter, Michael (Editor), *Scotland's True Heritage Pubs,* St Albans, CAMRA, 2007; *Real Heritage Pubs of Wales* (with Dunn, Mike), St Albans, CAMRA, 2010.

Smith, Steve (Editor), *Manchester Pub Guide,* St Albans, CAMRA, 2011.

Stapley, Fiona (Editor), *The Good Pub Guide 2016,* Ebury Press, 2015.

Strangest Books, *Strangest Pubs in Britain – Seeing is Believing,* Strangest Books, 2002.

Taylor, Donald F., *The Story of a Village Inn* (the Pack o' Cards), Combe Martin, self-published, undated.

Websites

www.huishepiscopi.org.uk, www.thamehistory.net and those mentioned on pages 138-139.

CAMRA's national online pub guide, www.whatpub.com, has been invaluable for finding out basic details of pubs in advance of visiting an area.

INDEX

The Fat Cat, Norwich.